Praise for
31 Verses to Write on Your Heart

"Liz Curtis Higgs has given us a versatile resource. Part story-rich devotional and part study-driven commentary, *31 Verses to Write on Your Heart* is as smart as it is approachable, as profound as it is practical. As someone who believes deeply in the importance of Scripture memorization but struggles with it all the same, I am personally grateful for this book."

—AMANDA BIBLE WILLIAMS, Chief Content Officer of She Reads Truth and coauthor of *Open Your Bible: God's Word Is for You and for Now*

"Consider *31 Verses to Write on Your Heart* your new spiritual strategy for deepening your daily walk with God. Full of relatable stories, this Scripture-saturated guide enables you to see familiar verses in a fresh, relevant way. Liz Curtis Higgs's clever tips tucked throughout will empower you to move from simply wishing you had time to memorize Scripture to actually inscribing God's precious Word forever on your heart. Whether you've walked with Jesus for decades—or just since last Tuesday—this encouraging and practical book will fertilize your soul."

—KAREN EHMAN, Proverbs 31 Ministries national speaker and *New York Times* best-selling author of *Keep It Shut*

"Liz writes just as she speaks: eloquently, accurately, and with power. And *31 Verses to Write on Your Heart* is no exception. With her signature style, Liz weaves biblical context, fresh insight, and practical application in a way that empowers, educates, and equips. And if we ever needed a deeper understanding of God's Word, ever needed His precious truths written on our hearts, it's now. It's today. Take this book, soak it up, and know God's Word for yourself."

—SUSIE LARSON, radio host of *Live the Promise* and author of *Your Powerful Prayers*

"Writing God's Word on our hearts is insurance. It's truth we can call on 24/7 in times of fear, insecurity, or intimidation. Liz, a faithful friend to all of us, has searched out truth and shared it by way of her brilliant mind and darling heart. Don't miss this chance for thirty-one days of life enrichment."

—PATSY CLAIRMONT, Women of Faith speaker, artist, and author of *You Are More Than You Know*

"Liz Curtis Higgs has a gift for taking important truths in Scripture and making them accessible, understandable, and easily digestible. In *31 Verses to Write on Your Heart,* Liz leads you through verses that are loved by countless numbers of believers. You will be inspired and encouraged to cherish God's Word through practical and personal tips for hiding His letter of love in your heart."

—CHRYSTAL EVANS HURST, coauthor of *Kingdom Woman*

Praise for
The Women of Christmas

"Breathtaking! *The Women of Christmas* is tender and joy filled and funny and faithful. With genuine warmth, profound wisdom, and refreshing wonder, Liz Curtis Higgs offers up a perfect seasonal blend—just what every woman in the midst of Christmas needs. I savored every word."

—ANN VOSKAMP, author of the *New York Times* bestseller *One Thousand Gifts: A Dare to Live Fully Right Where You Are*

"Liz Curtis Higgs ably mines the Scriptures, revealing undiscovered treasures in the familiar story. Through the pages of this powerful little book, we get to peer into the hearts of these women and find our own hearts melting at the beauty of God's grace."

—NANCY GUTHRIE, author of the Bible study series Seeing Jesus in the Old Testament

"This season delight your friends with an early gift of *The Women of Christmas,* inviting them to see how Elizabeth, Mary, and Anna were part of God's great plan to rescue us. As Liz puts it, 'Never doubt for a moment that women matter to the Almighty.'"

—DEE BRESTIN, author of *Idol Lies: Facing the Truth About Our Deepest Desires*

"*The Women of Christmas* invites us to steal away with our Savior during the hustle and bustle of one of the busiest seasons of the year. In her warm and welcoming voice, Liz Curtis Higgs draws us into the compelling stories of the women who surrounded our Messiah's birth and encourages us to consider our own relationship with Him. An inspirational and biblically rich devotional. What a wonderful way to experience Christmas!"

—KELLY MINTER, author of *Nehemiah: A Heart That Can Break*

31 Verses
TO WRITE ON YOUR
Heart

OTHER BOOKS BY LIZ CURTIS HIGGS

NONFICTION
Bad Girls of the Bible
Really Bad Girls of the Bible
Unveiling Mary Magdalene
Slightly Bad Girls of the Bible
Rise and Shine
Embrace Grace
My Heart's in the Lowlands
The Girl's Still Got It
The Women of Christmas
It's Good to Be Queen

CONTEMPORARY FICTION
Mixed Signals
Bookends
Mercy Like Sunlight

HISTORICAL FICTION
Thorn in My Heart
Fair Is the Rose
Whence Came a Prince
Grace in Thine Eyes
Here Burns My Candle
Mine Is the Night
A Wreath of Snow

CHILDREN'S
The Parable of the Lily
The Sunflower Parable
The Pumpkin Patch Parable
The Pine Tree Parable
Parable Treasury

Liz Curtis Higgs

Best-selling author of *The Women of Christmas*

31 Verses

TO WRITE ON YOUR

Heart

WATERBROOK

31 Verses to Write on Your Heart

All Scripture quotations, unless otherwise indicated, are taken from the Holy Bible, New International Version®, niv®. Copyright © 1973, 1978, 1984, 2011 by Biblica Inc.® Used by permission. All rights reserved worldwide. For a list of the additional Bible versions that are quoted, see page 203.

Hardcover ISBN 978-1-60142-891-2
eBook ISBN 978-1-60142-892-9

Copyright © 2016 by Liz Curtis Higgs

Cover design by Kelly L. Howard; photography by Georgianna Lane

Published in the United States by WaterBrook, an imprint of the Crown Publishing Group, a division of Penguin Random House LLC, New York.

WaterBrook® and its deer colophon are registered trademarks of Penguin Random House LLC.

Library of Congress Cataloging-in-Publication Data
Names: Higgs, Liz Curtis, author.
Title: 31 verses to write on your heart / Liz Curtis Higgs.
Other titles: Thirty-one verses to write on your heart
Description: First Edition. | Colorado Springs, Colorado : WaterBrook Press, 2016. |
    Includes bibliographical references.
Identifiers: LCCN 2016010338 (print) | LCCN 2016031385 (ebook) | ISBN
    9781601428912 (hardcover) | ISBN 9781601428929 (electronic)
Subjects: LCSH: Bible—Meditations.
Classification: LCC BS491.5 .H54 2016 (print) | LCC BS491.5 (ebook) | DDC
    242/.5—dc23
LC record available at https://lccn.loc.gov/2016010338

Printed in the United States of America
2018

10 9 8 7 6

Special Sales
Most WaterBrook books are available at special quantity discounts when purchased in bulk by corporations, organizations, and special-interest groups. Custom imprinting or excerpting can also be done to fit special needs. For information, please e-mail special marketscms@penguinrandomhouse.com or call 1-800-603-7051.

To Doris Foster,
my Kentucky mom,
who showed me how to be a
lifelong student of God's Word.
I love you, Doc.

Contents

Well Versed

*S*now was falling thick and fast across my windshield on a cold February night many winters ago. Not far ahead I saw the glowing lights of a bookstore.

Liz, you drove through a snowstorm to buy a book? I did. But it wasn't just any book.

Minutes earlier, seated in a toasty-warm office, I'd confessed my sins (well, most of them) to the pastor of a church I'd started attending. I told him enough to get my point across, to convince him I was a Bad Girl.

The pastor gently said, "So you've lived a worldly life."

I was confused. "No, I did all that stuff in America."

He smiled. Then he prayed and encouraged me to read the book of John.

I bolted out of his office, intent on buying a Bible right then, snow or no snow. When I arrived at the bookstore, the place was deserted, and the cashier was freaked out about the weather. But I found what I was looking for: the biggest, thickest study Bible in town.

Safely back home, I opened to the book of John and read "In the beginning was the Word."[1] Did this mean way back when God created the earth? No, even before that. "Before the world began, the Word was there."[2]

Clearly, God wasn't talking about a printed book. He was talking about the Living Word. His Son. *Wow.* That meant long before Jesus appeared as a baby in Bethlehem, He was with God.

I kept reading. "And the Word was with God, and the Word was God."[3] Right. Father and Son together with the Holy Spirit, bound throughout eternity. So much truth packed into a single verse. *Is the whole Bible like this?* I wondered.

Sitting there in my drafty old apartment, where central heat was little more than a rumor, I let the truth of John 1:1 sink in and was warmed by its poetic beauty and what it revealed about this God whom I was only beginning to understand.

Then I read the next verse. And the next. I inhaled the book of John, then Psalms, then the letters of Paul. I couldn't get enough, didn't want to stop.

With each passing month I feared that my enthusiasm for the Bible might wear thin. That once I'd read every page, the stories and lessons wouldn't be as exciting the second time, let alone the tenth time.

Now I know the truth. Whenever I read a familiar verse, God reveals a richer, deeper meaning. And when I find a passage I've not read before? Pure joy.

Is that how reading the Bible is for you? An ongoing journey of discovery, an endless adventure? Or has it become a duty, a task, something to be checked off your daily to-do list? Maybe it's not on your list at all and you're wondering why an ancient book has any significance in our modern world.

Here's why reading the Bible matters. When you spend time in God's Word, life starts making sense. The broken places inside you begin to heal. Darkness and discouragement give way to the light of hope. You have a new reason to get out of bed in the morning. Your purpose becomes clearer, and your desire to make a difference grows.

The Bible can do all that? It can. It will. Just begin. Go slowly. Stand on tiptoe, anticipating all God has in store for you. "I wait for the LORD, my whole being waits, and in his word I put my hope."[4]

We're about to look at thirty-one verses, each one carefully divided into phrases and then into individual words. We'll consider what God is saying and how we can apply His truth to our lives, starting today. "The word is very near you; it is in your mouth and in your heart so you may obey it."[5] That's where we want to land after reading, studying, and memorizing God's Word: we want to do what He asks of us.

If you've been reading the Bible for a few seasons, is there one verse you cherish above all others? A powerful statement that nourishes and sustains you year in and year out? Words you've posted on your fridge, stitched on fabric, written on greeting cards, included in your e-mail signature?

When I asked that question on social media, more than a thousand women responded with their favorite verses. I think you'll love the ones they've chosen, gathered here in no particular order simply because they all matter. Your personal pick may be among them, or you could discover a verse that calls your name and speaks to your current situation.

That's one of the beautiful things about the Bible: it meets us right where we are. Since "all Scripture is God-breathed,"[6] we can be sure every word is vital and every verse serves God's good purpose.

You might use *31 Verses to Write on Your Heart* as a daily devotional, reading through it in a month, following the Study Guide as you go. (You'll find that resource in the back of the book.) Or you could read five chapters each week and meet with a circle of friends to discuss what you're learning, perhaps over a six-week stretch. Whatever works for you . . . works!

If you're ready to give Scripture memorization a go, you'll see lots of practical ideas and fun tips scattered throughout the book, then collected in the final pages for easy reference. You'll also find a page at the end of each chapter where you can write your favorite translation of the verse to help you remember it word for word.

I know, I know. You don't have time. Your memory isn't what it used to be. You tried before and gave up. You think it's too hard. I get it. Totally.

Still, here's what the Bible says: "Keep my words and store up my commands within you."[7] This isn't simply the wisdom of King Solomon written to his son. This is the Word of God written for all of us. *Keep* and *store*. That's memorizing Scripture in a nutshell.

And look at all the benefits of having the Word in our hearts! First, we can share His truth with authority. Rather than our having to say, "Uh, let me find this for you in the Bible, because I know it's here somewhere," God tells us to "take hold of my words with all your heart"[8] so that our counsel is solid and effective. Unless we point people to Scripture, we're giving them little more than our opinion.

Second, when temptation knocks on our door, the verses we've memorized will come to our rescue. Countless times God's Word has stopped me in my tracks before I veered down the wrong path. The psalmist confessed, "I have hidden your word in my heart that I might not sin against you."[9] A good plan for all believers.

A third benefit? While we're learning these verses, our loved ones will be learning them with us. Saying verses aloud not only helps *us* remember them; it also helps anyone who hears them. "Impress them on your children. Talk about them when you sit at home and when you walk along the road, when you lie down and when you get up."[10]

Best of all, when God's Word is written on our hearts, it goes with us everywhere. Our smartphones and tablets may run out of juice, and even a small travel Bible can be out of reach when we need it most. God has a better plan: "These commandments that I give you today are to be on your hearts."[11] By memorizing key passages from His Word, we'll be ready to encourage others and give them hope.

So glad we're doing this together, beloved!

Write On, Sister

Let love and faithfulness never leave you;
bind them around your neck,
write them on the tablet of your heart.

PROVERBS 3:3

O pen the Bible to any page, and your eyes will land on truth. Every time. Our first verse describes how we can grasp those amazing truths and write them across the pages of our lives with indelible ink.

Let love and faithfulness never leave you; . . . *Proverbs 3:3*

From God's point of view, love and faithfulness are inseparable. One can't exist without the other. Because God loves us, He remains ever faithful. Because God is faith itself, His love is never ending.

Whether translated as "loyalty and kindness" (NLT) or "grace and truth" (CJB), two Hebrew words are used here: *chesed,* meaning "favor, mercy, lovingkindness," and *emeth,* meaning "firmness, faithfulness, truth."[1] Such concepts are drenched in goodness, sweet as honey, and deeply satisfying—the very opposite of "hatred and selfishness," of "hypocrisy or falsehood" (AMPC).

Sadly, we live in a world that often focuses on the negative. We harbor unkind feelings toward others. We insist on doing things our way and for our benefit. We call people two faced, even as we hide our own duplicity.

Some days even the best of us can act like the worst of us.

This proverb shows us the way out. "Don't lose your grip on Love and Loyalty" (MSG), and "do not lose sight of mercy and truth" (VOICE). How do we do that? We seek the Lord before we turn to an earthly friend, however wise. And we read His Word before we open another book, however edifying.

The Lord knows we can't drum up love and faithfulness on our own; that's why He weaves these righteous qualities into our very being. The love is all His, the loyalty is all His, yet both are threaded through us by His masterful design.

Our part? Holding His truths close to our hearts.

. . . bind them around your neck, . . . *Proverbs 3:3*

This phrase is so visual, so tactile. Imagine slipping God's sacred words onto a silver chain so you could "wear them like a necklace" (NCV), displaying His loyalty and kindness for all to see.

When I was twelve, my first crush gave me a wooden ring (*the* thing to wear that year). Because my fingers were too small for his ring, I wore it on a leather cord around my neck, proudly on display. That ring told the world I was chosen. That ring told me I was cherished. And that leather cord gently rubbing against my skin? A constant reminder of the one who mattered most to me.

Interesting thing about necklaces: they rest against the carotid artery, one of the most accurate places to measure a heartbeat. Maybe now is a good time to take our spiritual pulse and ask ourselves, *Does my heart truly beat for the Lord? Is His truth active in me?* If the answer is "Sometimes yes, sometimes no," then the rest of Proverbs 3:3 will show us how we can put God's words of love and faithfulness into practice every day, every hour.

. . . write them on the tablet of your heart. *Proverbs 3:3*

We have all sorts of tablets now, from spiral bound to sleek digital models with countless apps. But such tablets are easily broken, stolen, or lost forever. God asks us to store His wisdom in a more permanent place—"deep within" (NLT) on the "tables of thy heart" (DRA). The same Hebrew word describes "the tablets of stone inscribed by the finger of God"[2] that the Lord covered with His commandments and entrusted to Moses.

The tablets God writes on today aren't hard stones. They're tender hearts. He wants His truths etched "in your mind" (CEV) so you can "meditate on them" (VOICE). I'm grateful to have God's Word on my cell phone, my Kindle, my laptop, my bookshelf, but where it makes the most difference is in my heart.

As a writer, speaker, teacher, and, most of all, a woman who loves Jesus, this is my constant prayer: "May these words of my mouth and this meditation of my heart be pleasing in your sight, LORD, my Rock and my Redeemer."[3] When His loving words are in our minds, they are far more likely to pour out of our mouths.

As you reflect on Proverbs 3:3, how might you write His love and faithfulness across the heart of each person you meet today?

Lord, You've made this so simple
and so abundantly clear.
When I read Your Word,
when I study Your Word,
when I memorize Your Word,
when I live Your Word,
Your love and faithfulness
will beat in my heart so loudly
others may hear and see Your truth
and be set free.
Oh, let it be so, Lord!

His Word, Your Heart

> **Tip #1 for memorizing Scripture:**
> Pray. It's the most important step of all.

Proverbs 3:3 from the New International Version:

Let love and faithfulness never leave you;
bind them around your neck,
write them on the tablet of your heart.

Proverbs 3:3 from your favorite translation:

All New You

Therefore, if anyone is in Christ,
the new creation has come:
The old has gone, the new is here!

2 CORINTHIANS 5:17

Any verse with an exclamation point warms my heart, and especially this one—the first verse I memorized as a new believer. Season by season these life-changing words have become even dearer to me than when, with tears in my eyes, I read them for the first time.

Get ready, because 2 Corinthians 5:17 contains at least eight huge truths and in some translations *two* exclamation points!

Listen now for God's gentle voice.

Therefore, . . . *2 Corinthians 5:17*

Therefore is a summary word, taking into account all that came before it. This portion of the letter to the church at Corinth is about reconciliation. About being Christ's ambassadors. About looking at our sisters and brothers of the faith through a new lens.

Therefore says, "Because of all Christ did for us, consider this."

. . . if . . . 2 Corinthians 5:17

If is an open door, revealing endless possibilities and overflowing with hope. Jesus often used this word in His teaching: "if you have faith"[1] and "if you knew the gift of God"[2] and "if you remain in me."[3]

If makes us stop and ask, *Who is this verse meant for? Am I invited?*

. . . anyone . . . 2 Corinthians 5:17

Ah. *Anyone* definitely includes you, so this verse is yours to claim. Whether we're talking "any man" (asv) or "any person" (ampc), the pathway to eternal life is clearly lit, and the Lord Himself beckons us forward.

. . . is . . . 2 Corinthians 5:17

I know, I know. "*Is*, Liz? You're focusing on the word *is*?" Absolutely. It's the pivotal word in this verse. Either a person *is* or *is not* a follower of Christ. Though we are always growing in our faith, each of us has a defining moment when we see Jesus for who He is.

And that moment is defined by God, not by us.

When Jesus asked Peter, "Who do you say I am?" and Peter responded, "You are the Messiah, the Son of the living God," the Lord didn't congratulate Peter for being wise or clever. Instead, Jesus told him, "This was not revealed to you by flesh and blood, but by my Father in heaven."[4] Peter made his confession of faith by God's power alone.

I AM declares that I am. Not the other way around.

See why *is* really is such a big deal?

. . . in Christ, . . . 2 Corinthians 5:17

Some translations give the little word *in* a bit more muscle—"belongs to" (CEV), "united with" (CJB), "joined to" (GNT). The One in whom "we live and move and have our being"[5] is what matters, which is why the word *in* cannot stand alone.

We are *in Christ,* and He is in us. "The gift of God is eternal life *in Christ Jesus* our Lord."[6] Those are my italics, just to make the point. And again, "There is now no condemnation for those who are *in Christ Jesus.*"[7]

Dozens of verses illuminate this truth. The rest of 2 Corinthians 5:17 depends on the Lord's work *in us* now that we live *in Him.*

. . . the new creation has come: . . .
2 Corinthians 5:17

God doesn't just clean us up, fix us up, straighten us up. He re-creates us in the image of His Son. He starts from scratch. He makes us new. In Christ we become "a new being" (GNT), "a new person" (NLT), "a new creature altogether" (AMPC). In Christ we get "a fresh start" (MSG).

What does that look like in real life? There are as many answers as there are people. For me, a changed life decades ago looked like this:

- I stopped drinking alcohol and started going to church.
- I stopped using drugs and started reading the Bible.
- I stopped sleeping with strangers and started making real friends.
- I stopped running away and started putting down roots.
- I stopped pretending I had all the answers and started asking God questions.

Through it all God loved me. That was the realization that undid me, in the best sense of the word. It shattered my misconceptions. It trampled my pride.

God didn't just rock my world. God blew my world apart and then rebuilt it from the ground up.

> . . . The old has gone, . . . *2 Corinthians 5:17*

Truly it has. On the days you feel as if your spiritual roof is sagging and the walls are caving in, be confident of this: "He who began a good work in you will carry it on to completion until the day of Christ Jesus."[8] Some of us start well and then run out of steam. Our God is a starter *and* a finisher, so He helps us with both.

First, the icky stuff from our old lives must be pried from our stubborn hands and cast aside. Old habits, old ideas, old lies. My inclination is to tuck such things into the deep recesses of a drawer. Just in case I need them later. Just in case I miss them. God has a better plan. He makes certain those old things have truly "gone away" (CEB) and "the past is forgotten" (CEV).

Gone means gone. History. Out of sight, out of mind, out of reach. Gone means good riddance. Really good.

> . . . the new is here! *2 Corinthians 5:17*

See how the zippy exclamation point grabs our attention? The Greek word *idou* here is also rendered "behold" (ASV), "see" (NRSV), and my favorite, "Lo!" (WYC). Getting rid of the old would be exciting enough, yet God also brings in the new. A new gift, a new talent, a new calling.

When God turned my world right-side up, I was working at a radio station and could never have imagined speaking at conferences or writing books or teaching the Bible. Hiding in a broadcasting studio, I felt safe, invisible.

But . . .

God said, "The fresh and new has come!" (AMPC).

God said, "A new life has begun!" (NLT).

What is God saying to you, beloved? Is it time to put aside something old? To let go, to walk away? Even now He is bringing new life to your doorstep.

Make Him welcome. Let Him in.

To be in Christ—
that's all You asked of me, Lord,
and all that You require.
You sweep away the old.
You usher in the new.
I'm beyond grateful that
You made something
from my nothing.

His Word, Your Heart

Tip #2 for memorizing Scripture:
Memorize the reference, then the verse,
and then repeat the reference.

2 Corinthians 5:17 from the New International Version:

Therefore, if anyone is in Christ,
the new creation has come:
The old has gone, the new is here!

2 Corinthians 5:17 from your favorite translation:

3

Afraid Not

Fear of man will prove to be a snare,
but whoever trusts in the LORD is kept safe.

PROVERBS 29:25

*I*f the phrase "What will people think?" ever spills from your lips, here's the truth: what people think about us can't compare to what our Savior thinks about us.

Fear of man . . . *Proverbs 29:25*

Fear is the right and natural response when our safety is threatened. But what we're talking about here is "the fear of human opinion" (MSG). Disparaging comments, withering looks, derisive laughter, arched eyebrows—all the unkind ways people communicate that we don't measure up, that we have *FAILURE* stamped on our foreheads.

When we're on the receiving end of judgmental opinions, our response is often "anxiety" (EXB). The Hebrew word *charadah* describes it as "trembling violently." For me it's a knot in the pit of my stomach. For others it might be a pounding heart or damp forehead.

However much we pretend people's opinions don't matter to us, they *do* matter—often because we're looking in the wrong direction for approval. That's why "it is dangerous to be concerned with what others think" (GNT).

What if they think terrible things about us? Or (horrors!) what if they don't think about us at all? Fear becomes a cage from which we can't escape.

> . . . will prove to be a snare, . . . *Proverbs 29:25*

When we fear what others think of us, we become "trapped" (CEB). We do things that make us *look* good rather than things that *are* good. We focus on pleasing people instead of pleasing the Lord.

The first weekend I spoke at a Women of Faith conference, I was a nervous wreck. I bought *two* new outfits, went shopping for boots, got a fancy manicure, and tried a new hair salon. "Mom, what's the deal?" my daughter wanted to know. "You never obsess over this stuff."

I knew exactly what the deal was. Unfortunately, it had nothing to do with the audience *or* the Lord I was there to serve. It was the other speakers. *Will they like me? Will I fit in? Will I look like I belong on the team?* Good grief. You would have thought I was going to a junior high slumber party. All my anxiety turned out to be a waste of good deodorant because my speaking sisters welcomed me with open arms, even before they saw the cute boots.

Putting too much stock in the opinions of others can get us into trouble because some people are never truly pleased or fully appeased. Whatever we do for them and however well we perform, they still can't give us what our hearts need most: genuine love, utter peace, and the heavenly assurance of "Well done, good and faithful servant!"[1]

People pleasing "disables" (MSG) us. It makes us less hopeful, less useful, and definitely less joyful. It keeps us from sharing our love for God because we're not walking in love. We're walking in fear.

The apostle Paul posed these challenging questions: "Am I now trying to win the approval of human beings, or of God? Or am I trying to please people? If I were still trying to please people, I would not be a servant of Christ."[2]

The phrase "if I were still trying" suggests Paul took the people-pleasing route at some point in his life, perhaps before he knew the Lord or in the early years of his ministry. Finally Paul got over himself. Got over wanting to please others. Got his head on straight about what matters and who matters.

Following Paul's example, we can turn away from the deathtrap of public opinion and turn to the One worth trusting, worth pleasing.

. . . but whoever trusts in the LORD . . . *Proverbs 29:25*

In this verse the word *but* gets us ready for good news: the joy of no longer fretting "What will people think?" And the word *whoever* is an invitation. Say yes, my friend. This promise is for anyone who "leans on, trusts in, and puts his confidence in the Lord" (AMPC).

The Lord knows our needs and will surely meet them. Not our longing for applause, which builds our pride, but our need for His acceptance, which brings us peace. Not our wish to be popular, which has little value, but our deep need to be loved, His richest gift to us.

On the days when trust wanes and fears rise, see if speaking these truths aloud restores your confidence in our trustworthy God:

- "I trust in God's unfailing love for ever and ever."[3]
- "In God I trust and am not afraid. What can man do to me?"[4]
- "I will say of the LORD, 'He is my refuge and my fortress, my God, in whom I trust.'"[5]

Trusting Him drives away our fears. Seeking Him assures our safety.

... is kept safe. *Proverbs 29:25*

For me, the word *safe* is full of images and childhood memories. Bird-watching in the woods with my big brother, Tom. Snuggling beneath my bedcovers with a flashlight so I could read a bit longer. Finding my mama bent over her flower garden on summer afternoons. More recently, curling up on the couch with my hubby and kitties while watching *Downton Abbey* on PBS.

Safe. Warm. Familiar.

But the Hebrew word *sagab,* often translated "safe," literally means "to be (inaccessibly) high." Out of the enemy's reach. "Protected" (HCSB) and utterly "secure" (CEB). "Lifted up" (JUB) well "above danger" (CJB).

The psalmist declares, "The LORD will keep you from all harm—he will watch over your life."[6] He holds us above the fray. High and lifted up, we no longer need to fear what people might think, say, or do. They can't touch us, literally or figuratively.

That's why we can rest in this truth, certain of the answer: "If God is for us, who can be against us?"[7] No one.

Lord, I choose to trust Your opinion
rather than letting others define me.
Knowing You will always love and protect me,
I can reach out to help others,
affirming instead of assessing,
giving instead of taking,
loving instead of judging.

His Word, Your Heart

Tip #3 for memorizing Scripture:
Pick a good place.
It helps to do memory work
in consistent surroundings.

Proverbs 29:25 from the New International Version:

Fear of man will prove to be a snare,
but whoever trusts in the Lord is kept safe.

Proverbs 29:25 from your favorite translation:

4

Great Expectations

*"For I know the plans I have for you," declares the L*ORD,
"plans to prosper you and not to harm you,
plans to give you hope and a future."

JEREMIAH 29:11

A favorite of many believers, this verse is empowering, encouraging, and rich with promise. It's been captured in stained glass, painted on canvas, carved in wood, silkscreened on T-shirts, etched in metal, embossed on greeting cards, and printed on posters.

Eager to embrace such good news, we often skip over the verses leading up to this one. Fact is, this declaration followed the *worst news* the prophet Jeremiah could have written to the people of God exiled in Babylon!

Here's the story: After the fall of Jerusalem and the destruction of the temple in 586 BC,[1] King Nebuchadnezzar marched God's people off to Babylon as captives. The Lord was fine with that. All part of His plan.

But a false prophet named Hananiah told the Israelites they wouldn't be held captive long and prosperity was right around the corner. Then

Jeremiah lowered the boom and informed the Israelites, in essence, "No way, people. Make yourselves at home in Babylon. You'll be held in bondage there for seventy years."

Seventy years? You can bet that wasn't what they wanted to hear. It meant most of them would spend their entire lives in exile and a great number would die there. The psalmist wrote, "Our days may come to seventy years, or eighty, if our strength endures."[2] Even today the average life expectancy in the United States is just seventy-eight years.

Then in Jeremiah 29:10 the Lord assured His people, "When seventy years are completed for Babylon, I will come to you and fulfill my good promise to bring you back to this place." Something to look forward to, then, even if it was a lifetime away. Even if the promise was for their children and grandchildren and not for them.

What Jeremiah shared next were God's marvelous plans for Israel's future as a nation. But in the meantime the people's lives would be filled with difficulties and disappointments. God didn't pretend otherwise.

For the Israelites in Babylon, those seventy hard years weren't without purpose. Whatever situation we're stuck in right now isn't meaningless either. As beloved commentator Matthew Henry wrote, "Let them not sorrow as those that have no hope, no joy; for they have both."[3]

Why do we have hope? Joy? Peace? Because our story isn't finished yet.

"For I know . . ." *Jeremiah 29:11*

A gentle but firm reminder from God: "I know what I'm doing" (MSG). When the One who created the heavens and the earth says, "I know," He's not kidding. "The LORD is a God who knows."[4] Again from Matthew Henry: "We often do not know our own thoughts, nor know our own mind, but God is never at any uncertainty within himself."[5]

I'm elated when I meet people who know what they're talking about on a given subject. Their skill and knowledge are a great comfort. Whatever you ask them, they answer with the confidence of education and experience.

Now imagine a God who knows everything there is to know. Especially One who "knows all human plans"[6] and "knows those who are his."[7] Our God knows us deeply. Loves us dearly. And promises us He has things well in hand.

> "... the plans I have for you," ... *Jeremiah 29:11*

Literally, it's "the plans that I am planning" (LEB) or "the thoughts that I think" (ASV). It's the same word—first as a noun, then as a verb. In Hebrew it's a delicious mouthful—*machashabah,* which means "thought" or "device." Sometimes the word suggests a bad intention or purpose, like a nefarious plot. Other times it's a delightful surprise in the making.

God isn't tipping His hand, giving away what's to come. He just wants us to know, "I have it all planned out" (MSG). In other words, "Trust Me. I've got this" (LRV: Lizzie Revised Version).

> ... declares the LORD, ... *Jeremiah 29:11*

Jeremiah wanted to be sure the people exiled in Babylon understood that this message came straight from God. "This is the LORD's declaration" (HCSB), he told them. It's "an affirmation of Jehovah" (YLT).

The prophet wasn't hiding behind God's cloak. He wasn't afraid of the people. He simply wanted to honor the Lord and direct all their attention toward Him.

> ... "plans to prosper you ..." *Jeremiah 29:11*

God was thinking "thoughts of peace" (ASV) concerning His people. He had plans for their "well-being" (CJB), for their "security" (EXB). Prosperity would come again but only according to His timetable.

Growing up, I heard this message: "Don't wait around for some man to take care of you. Earn your own living; create your own security." So I did what young women of my generation were expected to do. I climbed ladders and broke through glass ceilings. Sadly, God and His Word weren't the rungs beneath my feet. Only when I realized my ladder was propped against the wrong building was I ready to admit I needed a far better plan than mine.

The word translated "prosper" is the familiar Hebrew word *shalom,* which assures us of "completeness, soundness, welfare, peace." Rather than shame, God offered His people *shalom.* It's a word often spoken in the streets and houses of Jerusalem today, meant as a greeting, a blessing, a wish for better days.

> "... and not to harm you, ..." *Jeremiah 29:11*

Unlike *shalom, ra'a'* is a Hebrew word that encompasses every form of badness or evil—"adversity, affliction, calamity, displeasure, distress"—whether natural or moral. However dire things appeared, Jeremiah was assuring God's people He didn't "plan to hurt" (ERV) them. "Torment" (WYC) was not on the menu, and He would surely "not abandon" (MSG) them.

God's plans for Israel were for their own good. Harm was the last thing He had in mind. Hope was where He was headed.

> "... plans to give you hope ..." *Jeremiah 29:11*

That word *plan* is getting a real workout in this verse, isn't it? The Lord knows how desperately we make lists and then toss them out, how we fret over our calendars, how we agonize over whether we'll get everything done.

Again—still—God had "welfare and peace" (AMPC) earmarked for His people. He promised, "I will bless you with a future filled with hope" (CEV). And hope does not disappoint, not when our hope is in God. *Tiqvah,* the Hebrew word for "hope" or "expectation" in this verse, literally means a "cord," something a believer can hang on to.

". . . and a future." *Jeremiah 29:11*

This life is a shadow, a whisper, no more significant than the turning of a page. The Lord "set eternity in the human heart"[8] so people would gaze beyond the here and now. When God said, "I shall give you a good ending" (WYC), He didn't mean they would die peacefully in their sleep. He told them "your final outcome" (AMPC) will be "the future you hope for" (GNT), "the end that you wait for" (JUB). The God who spoke these words to Israel centuries ago is the same God who has made plans for us as well. "And this is what he promised us—eternal life."[9]

How might committing this verse to memory help you on those hard days when you, too, feel as if you're stuck in Babylon?

Heavenly Father, You hold my future.
That's all I need to know.
Every moment, every detail
is in Your hands.

His Word, Your Heart

> **Tip #4 for memorizing Scripture:**
> Choose the best time of day,
> when your mind is at its sharpest.

Jeremiah 29:11 from the New International Version:

"For I know the plans I have for you," declares the LORD,
"plans to prosper you and not to harm you,
plans to give you hope and a future."

Jeremiah 29:11 from your favorite translation:

5

Start Smart

The fear of the LORD is the beginning of wisdom,
and knowledge of the Holy One is understanding.

PROVERBS 9:10

*W*ho doesn't love the idea of being wise? Yet the first step toward wisdom is an unexpected one: fear. The kind of fear
that makes us fall down on our faces and tremble in God's holy presence.
If we long to be spiritually smart, this is where we start.

The fear of the LORD . . . *Proverbs 9:10*

God-fearing is a phrase we don't often hear anymore. Sounds a bit
dated. Old school. We'd rather focus on loving God and being loved by
Him. His love is a glorious truth, but it's not the first thing we need to
learn.

Instead, this is God's lesson plan:

- "Come, my children, listen to me; I will teach you the fear
  of the LORD."[1]

- "The fear of the Lord is pure, enduring forever."[2]
- "Now fear the Lord and serve him with all faithfulness."[3]

What does this kind of fear look like? "Respect" (cev). "Awe" (exb). "Reverence" (voice). We stand in wonder, we kneel in worship, and we live in obedience because of our holy and humble fear of the Almighty One.

God wants us to harbor a genuine fear of His mighty power and infinite strength. As the psalmist wrote, "If only we knew the power of your anger! Your wrath is as great as the fear that is your due."[4]

No one but God can rightly say, "I brought you into this world, and I can take you out." He did bring us in, beloved, and He will take us out, according to His perfect timing and because of His perfect love.

But for those of us with daddy issues, the idea of fearing God the Father may lead our thoughts in altogether the wrong direction. Not toward reverence, but dread.

When I was fourteen, my dad slapped me. I was mouthing off (there's a surprise), and he was furious. *So* furious he ran out of words.

My father loved me. He did. But the sting of that slap didn't feel like love. If you know firsthand what I'm talking about, your memories may go much deeper and be much darker than one angry slap on an ordinary school night.

As a new Christian reading "We have all had human fathers who disciplined us and we respected them for it,"[5] I felt my face grow hot. *Respect* wasn't the word that came to mind. *Fear* was what I felt. Anger. Resentment. And a deep sadness.

It took me a long time to warm to the idea of calling the Lord "*Abba,* Father."[6] The words were so personal, so trusting, so tender and intimate. *Abba,* in Aramaic. *Daddy,* at our house. *If I feared God, could I also love Him? Look up to Him? Fully trust Him?*

Yes. God is good and loving and worthy of our trust. And He shows us what a healthy fear of Him produces. Something wonderful, something new.

. . . is the beginning of wisdom, . . . Proverbs 9:10

Don't you love fresh starts? A new journal, a calendar without anything scribbled on it, a blank to-do list. For many of us "the chief and choice part" (AMPC) is "the start" (LEB).

God's grace is all about starting over. Being washed clean. Being made new. Since "his mercies begin afresh each morning,"[7] we can start right now—right where we are—to show the Lord more reverence, more honor, more awe. Truth is, "if you want to become wise, you must begin by respecting the LORD" (NIrV).

Anytime I lose sight of just how truly powerful God is, I read four short chapters in the Bible, Job 38–41, which begin with God's thunderous challenge to Job: "Where were you when I laid the earth's foundation?"[8] At the Higgs house we are so familiar with this passage that we simply say "Where were you . . . ," and a healthy fear of the Lord quickly keeps our pride in check.

. . . and knowledge of the Holy One . . . Proverbs 9:10

The Hebrew word *qadosh* means "sacred" or "holy." It's plural here, which is why some translators wrote of "holy things" (GNV) and "Holy Ones" (YLT). God is Father, Son, and Holy Spirit. We want to know all of Him, the whole of Him, the Holy of Him. Everything our minds can handle. Everything our hearts can hold.

We not only need to "learn about" (NLV) the Lord; we truly "must know" (CEV) Him. A relationship with our Creator and Savior is deeply personal and extends way beyond head knowledge.

It took me forever to understand this.

I heard about God for the first twenty-seven years of my life. Then I finally knew God—or, rather, I realized I was known by Him. All at once distance was replaced with intimacy. Cold indifference became

Spirit-fueled adoration. "Go away!" turned into "Please don't leave me or forsake me!"

He has never done so, and He never will.

. . . is understanding. *Proverbs 9:10*

This is where fear of the Lord takes us: understanding. Our destination is a deeper "insight into life" (MSG), which inevitably "results in good judgment" (NLT). Fear, respect, honor, worship, and reverence not only open the gateway to understanding His Word and His will, but they also result "in every other kind of understanding" (TLB).

Imagine all that goodness from putting into practice one four-letter word: *fear.*

Now take a moment to consider: What will this day look like if you remain in awe of the Lord, never forgetting who He is or what He can do?

Heavenly Father,
let it never be said of me, or of any of us,
"There is no fear of God before their eyes."[9]
When I read Your Word, fill my mind with wonder.
When I see Your creation, fill my heart with awe.
When You pour out Your mercy on me,
fill my soul with gratitude
and, yes, a healthy fear
of Your power and might.

His Word, Your Heart

Tip #5 for memorizing Scripture:
Set an alarm to remind you
to review your verse.

Proverbs 9:10 from the New International Version:

The fear of the LORD
is the beginning of wisdom,
and knowledge of the Holy One
is understanding.

Proverbs 9:10 from your favorite translation:

6

Can Do

I can do all this through him
who gives me strength.

PHILIPPIANS 4:13

In February 1943 a poster appeared on the walls of Westinghouse Electric to encourage women who'd been hired during the war effort. It was used only in-house and was gone after two weeks. The image of a muscular woman wearing a blue work shirt and red bandanna with the speech bubble "We Can Do It!" above her head wasn't rediscovered until the early 1960s when the women's movement claimed the image as their own.

Since then we've seen her everywhere—on postage stamps, coffee mugs, T-shirts, you name it.[1] In fact, this decades-old poster is still one of the ten most-requested images from the National Archives.[2]

So should we write "Philippians 4:13" across the bottom of this poster and hang it in our homes? Is a can-do attitude worth aiming for?

Or might that kind of thinking steer us in the wrong direction? Let's take a look.

I can do all this . . . *Philippians 4:13*

Sounds like the world's shortest motivational speech, and it's often used that way by believers as we jump to our feet and declare loudly and proudly, "I can do all things" (CJB).

Sure seems like a good frame of mind, right? Upbeat. Confident. Goal driven. The Greek word *ischuó* means "I am strong." Your Bible may say "I am ready" (AMP), "I am able" (HCSB), or "I can endure" (CEB). Can-do people are resourceful, with a positive attitude marked by joy-filled enthusiasm.

Is that a bad thing? Not at all. It just isn't necessarily a God thing. We get so excited about claiming, "I can do everything!" that we risk forgetting the One whose sacrifice makes that possible.

Rather than assuring the new believers at Philippi they could survive on their own, the apostle Paul was communicating to them—and to us—just the opposite. The only way we can manage life is through Christ. It's the Lord who can do "anything" (CEV) and indeed "all things" (KJV). So how did Paul handle life's ups and downs? He "learned to be content whatever the circumstances."[3]

Content? *Hmm.* Even those of us who know God's Word and love Him with all our hearts would probably admit we aren't 100 percent content. Nor do we happily embrace the verse that follows: "I know what it is to be in need, and I know what it is to have plenty. I have learned the secret of being content in any and every situation, whether well fed or hungry, whether living in plenty or in want."[4]

Well fed and living in plenty is today's lifestyle of choice.

Hungry and in want? Not if we can help it.

In my early twenties I worked three jobs at once and donated plasma for cash, trying to make ends meet. But I was hardly living in want. I had a roof (albeit leaky) over my head, an old VW parked at the curb, and on some weekends a bag of fresh vegetables from a friend's garden.

Even so, I wasn't content. I wanted more and was determined to get it.

Only a person like Paul, who'd "been there," could say "done that." When Paul declared, "I can do everything" (NLT), he also made it clear where his strength came from.

. . . through him . . . *Philippians 4:13*

This crucial truth is buried in the middle of the verse, like a treasure waiting to be discovered. Some translations get more specific—"by the power of Christ" (NIrv) and "through the Anointed One" (VOICE)—but the original Greek just says "in the one."

Why didn't Paul mention the Lord at the start of the verse—"Through Christ I can do everything"—so we'd be sure to get it right? Perhaps it's because Paul always talked about, wrote about, and preached about Jesus. Paul's letters have no other theme but "the One" (MSG).

. . . who gives me strength. *Philippians 4:13*

God's power and might sustained Paul. God's love and mercy kept him going. God's strength is a gift to all of us. We can't earn it or buy it; we can only receive it and acknowledge the One who gave it to us: "Christ gives me the strength to face anything" (CEV).

And His strength is enough. More than sufficient. Far beyond plenty. The Lord doesn't simply encourage us; He "infuses" (AMP) us.

"We Can Do It!" can be more than a war slogan. It's a cry for victory in the midst of our spiritual battles. A proclamation shout to the Enemy of our souls: "God is 'the One who makes me who I am'" (MSG).

Think what might happen if today you changed "I can do all things" to "God can do all things."

You truly are a can-do God.
And You alone make me a can-do woman.
Help me remember and acknowledge that
You are the source of my strength.
I can't do life without You.
But through You,
oh, what I can do!

His Word, Your Heart

Tip #6 for memorizing Scripture:
Decide on the best translation for you.

Philippians 4:13 from the New International Version:
I can do all this through him
who gives me strength.

Philippians 4:13 from your favorite translation:

7

Safe Guard

Above all else, guard your heart,
for everything you do flows from it.

PROVERBS 4:23

An old hope chest from my parents' attic holds a wealth of memories, including a dozen marble composition books that contain my earliest attempts at writing novels. However amateurish they are, I still treasure them. When my childhood home was dismantled and sold, that chest full of stories was all I asked for, all I wanted.

What's the most precious thing you own? The one possession that matters above everything else? Keep that in mind as we learn what God cherishes most.

Above all else, . . . *Proverbs 4:23*

Above all else, our society values beauty, wealth, fame, stuff. The visible, the temporal.

Above all else, our God values the hearts of His people. The unseen, the eternal.

That's why He calls us to take care of our inner selves, the place that harbors the Holy Spirit. A sacred space not meant for intruders.

... *guard your heart,* ... *Proverbs 4:23*

It's not a suggestion. It's a command: "Keep your heart pure" (NLV). Seriously, Lord? Pure? In this culture? We'd have to turn off our televisions, avoid our computers, skip the movies, stop reading the paper—

Wait. That's not what Jesus asked His followers to do.

He said to His Father, "As you sent me into the world, I have sent them into the world."[1] As long as we're here, this world is where we're meant to be. Although we are surrounded by constant temptations and pulled this way and that by our selfish desires, we are called and equipped by God to choose wisely.

Rather than view this as a protective verse to hide behind, think of it as a proactive verse to put into practice. By the power of the Holy Spirit, you can "protect your mind" (CEB) and "guard your thoughts" (CEV).

The Hebrew word *leb* means our "inner man, mind, will, heart." Not the fist-sized organ beating in our chests, but the place where we feel and think and seek after God.

Here's why your heart is so important to Him:

- It's where you store His Word. "Lay up his words in your heart."[2]
- It's where you respond to His invitation. "Love the LORD your God with all your heart."[3]
- It's where you learn to trust Him. "Trust in the LORD with all your heart."[4]

With our hearts safely in His hands, our lives flow in the right direction.

. . . for everything you do . . . Proverbs 4:23

All the "important things of life" (NLV), all the "issues" (ASV) we're wrapped up in, all the "consequences" (CJB) of our actions begin in our hearts.

Like the big Christmas gift I ordered for my husband, Bill. The one he fussed at me for giving him. It came straight from my heart—not to win his favor, but to show Bill how much I love him.

In a similar way God cherishes our heartfelt devotion. We're no longer trying to earn His favor, His mercy, His grace. We already have that and we know it. God has given us what we need most: His Son, who is more than enough, and His grace, which is more than sufficient.

Our gifts to the Lord—our worship, honor, and obedience—spring from our love for Him, a love that cannot be contained. Like "wellsprings" (OJB), the love in our hearts overflows its banks. Spilling out, it creates a stream that "determines the course" (NLT) our lives will follow.

We don't decide our future. We just decide who to love.

. . . flows from it. Proverbs 4:23

A broad, rushing stream in the Highlands of Scotland doesn't question its source or worry about its course. It simply flows. The water "cometh forth" (WYC) and goeth. (Sometimes the English major in me longeth to speaketh like that.)

Flow is a wonderful thing. Every minute of every hour our beating hearts send blood through our bodies, keeping us alive. We don't have to think about it. We don't have to plot, plan, or practice. It just flows.

Each time we love and trust instead of fret and fuss, God changes our stop-and-go into flow. What might you start doing—or stop doing—to keep your heart pure so God's love can pour through you?

However long it takes, Lord,
hide Your Word in my heart
until it beats purely for You.
Stand guard over
my thoughts, my words,
my actions, and my reactions
until everything that flows through me
honors You.

His Word, Your Heart

> ### Tip #7 for memorizing Scripture:
> Learn one verse at a time.

Proverbs 4:23 from the New International Version:

Above all else,
guard your heart,
for everything you do flows from it.

Proverbs 4:23 from your favorite translation:

Conversion
More than anything you guard, protect
your mind, life flows from it

Be careful how you think,
your life is shaped by your
thoughts. (Good news!

8

Blown Away

For the Spirit God gave us does not make us timid,
but gives us power, love and self-discipline.

2 TIMOTHY 1:7

When discussions turn to the Holy Spirit, some believers get a little nervous. Others become really excited. And many just scratch their heads. This verse gives us a crystal-clear, nonthreatening, yet full-throttle sense of the Spirit's role in our lives.

For the Spirit God gave us . . . *2 Timothy 1:7*

The Greek word *pneuma* means "spirit, wind, breath," telling us that God breathes life into us through His Spirit. Just as a body can't live without air, a believer can't live without the Holy Spirit. "The spirit . . . bestowed on us" (KNOX) shows the world we belong to Him.

Far more than a bride slipping on a wedding band or a baseball player wearing a team uniform, "when you believed, you were marked in him with a seal, the promised Holy Spirit."[1]

A permanent marker. An unbreakable seal.

This one is mine.

The Word assures us, "God's love has been poured out into our hearts through the Holy Spirit, who has been given to us."[2] The Spirit is a gift—unearned and undeserved—from the One who knows that our wobbly faith will require constant proof of His love, His acceptance, His grace, His affection.

Before He tells us what the Holy Spirit does, God reminds us what the Spirit doesn't do.

. . . does not make us timid, . . . *2 Timothy 1:7*

This is the only verse in the Bible that uses the Greek word *deilia,* meaning "reticence." "Timid" might be too soft a word. We're talking "terror" (ojb) and "dread" (wyc).

Icy hands. Weak knees. Tight throats.

The Holy Spirit "is not one that shrinks from danger" (knox). He doesn't leave us "craven and cringing" (ampc), and He "doesn't make cowards out of us" (cev). No, beloved. He takes away that "spirit of fearfulness" (asv) and makes us strong, brave, and unafraid.

. . . but gives us power, . . . *2 Timothy 1:7*

When we belong to God and are filled with His Spirit, we're no longer running on our power. We're running on His power. The Greek word *dunamis* means "miraculous power, might, strength." Think dynamite, with all its explosive energy.

If we're naturally timid, reticent, or shy, the idea of being "bold" (msg) or having "a spirit of action" (knox) might be thrilling. Or it might be unnerving. Will we suddenly turn into wild women? Speak out at business meetings? Approach strangers on the street?

Relax. With the Holy Spirit as your "source of power" (erv), you can be sure whatever He prompts and enables you to do will be for your good and for God's glory.

. . . love . . . *2 Timothy 1:7*

There are several words for *love* in the Bible. This one is *agapé,* a love centered in moral preference. God doesn't love you because He has to but because He chooses to. It's not duty but desire on His part.

God desires you? Yes, He does.

His love gives us the ability to love others in Jesus's name, not simply because it's the right thing to do, but because we genuinely care about people. God's love for them pours through us, refreshing us as we refresh others.

The Holy Spirit makes us not only emotionally and spiritually strong but mentally and practically strong as well.

. . . and self-discipline. *2 Timothy 1:7*

Don't panic about that first bit—"self." It's the Spirit who "helps us control ourselves" (NIrv). That's why "we have this treasure in jars of clay to show that this all-surpassing power is from God and not from us."[3]

The Greek word *sóphronismos,* used only in this verse, means "wise discretion." With the Spirit at work in us, we're "sensible" (MSG) and "well-balanced" (AMP) with "a sound mind" (GNV) and "good judgment" (EXB).

Alas, there are times when the flesh runs roughshod over the Spirit, and discipline goes out the window. Mind if I share one of those?

While speaking at a Christian writers conference, I stepped into the business center of the hotel to print out my notes. Both computers were occupied. A writing sister sat at one, and a gentleman I didn't recognize was winding up things at the other.

As he gathered his papers, I said in a cheery voice, "All finished, brother?"

"Brother?" he snarled and then started for the door in a huff.

Oops. Clearly not part of our group. "Sorry!" I called after him, trying to explain myself. "I was thinking *brother* sounded friendlier than *sir*. Or *mister*. Or *buddy*." When he didn't acknowledge me and banged the door shut behind him, I shouted out what I was really thinking. "Or *jerk*!"

My feathers still ruffled, I dropped onto the chair, hoping he hadn't heard me, only to realize that my Christian sister had heard and seen it all.

She smiled. "Glad to know you're human, Liz."

"Oh, I'm human, all right." *Groan.*

So what's the deal here? If the Holy Spirit lives in us, strengthening our faith, filling us with love for others, giving us discernment and good judgment, what was that about?

That was about letting my sin nature step forward in a big, messy, on-display way. The Holy Spirit doesn't desert us, but He does allow us to experience the consequences of our sin. Whether the man heard me or not really isn't the point. The attitude of my heart and the sharpness of my words were the problem.

Humbled by my foolishness, I asked the woman's forgiveness and the Lord's forgiveness and shared the story with the audience that night as an example of what not to do. Had I been able to track down the man, I would have apologized to him as well.

Did I learn a valuable lesson? You bet. Is that my favorite method of education? Not for one minute. Will that experience leap to mind next time I'm tempted to be unkind? Oh yes.

Why use a negative illustration for such a positive verse? Because if you experience a moment of weakness in the near future, I want you to know that you're not alone and that the Holy Spirit is still in charge. In fact, more in charge than ever as He uses our mistakes to teach us what grace and mercy look like up close.

What I call embarrassing, Lord,
You call a teachable moment.
Thank You for not only forgiving me
but also empowering me
to share Your love
through the Holy Spirit.

His Word, Your Heart

> **Tip #8 for memorizing Scripture:**
> Start with one verse a week.

2 Timothy 1:7 from the New International Version:

For the Spirit God gave us does not make us timid,
but gives us power, love and self-discipline.

fills

2 Timothy 1:7 from your favorite translation:

wise
discretion
good
judgment.
sound
mind

plug in to the spirit.

9

God Works

*And we know that in all things God works
for the good of those who love him,
who have been called according to his purpose.*

ROMANS 8:28

*Y*ou knew it was coming. Hardly a sermon goes by without a mention of this verse. People nod at the opening words. *Right. Got this one.* We've listened to it so many times we may no longer hear it at all.

Let's pretend we've never met this verse before. Come at it fresh. Have open minds. Consider that God might show us something we've missed all those other times. Just as His mercies are new every morning, so are His truths.

In the New International Version, this verse comes under the heading "Present Suffering and Future Glory." When we're suffering, the future may look bleak, even frightening. So the Lord addresses our greatest fear straight up. The tough situation we're in that seems permanent and meaningless is, in fact, temporary and purposeful.

And we know that . . . *Romans 8:28*

"We are well assured" (KNOX), Paul wrote, and "are confident" (VOICE) that the hardship we're dealing with today will end—and end well—because God is in it from start to finish.

. . . in all things . . . *Romans 8:28*

That's right, "everything" (CJB) we are up against, "every detail in our lives" (MSG), is not only on His radar. It's also in His hands. We were thinking God cares only about the big stuff. Not true. If it matters to us, it matters to God. We can pray about all of it, trust Him with all of it, and know He's got all of it.

What's on your list of major concerns right now? That stuff you're fretting about, obsessing over, suffering through? Go ahead; count them. Is it your finances? Your health? Your child? Your parents? Your job? Your church? Your marriage? Your singleness? Your friendships? Your future?

Whether you counted your difficulties on one hand or needed a calculator to keep track, they are all in His grip. *All.* Saying it again: *All things.*

And God isn't just holding them. He is doing something about them.

. . . God works . . . *Romans 8:28*

There it is. The assurance we need most. God is working on it. He labors on our behalf and gets the job done. Always.

Like a master auto mechanic, the Lord understands how all those parts under the hood work. After all, He made us according to His design. And He knows how to keep things running even when we're almost out of fuel and the road ahead is full of potholes.

Unlike the mechanic who takes a lunch break and goes home at night, "God is always at work" (CEV). His shop never closes. He adjusts and tightens and lubricates and runs diagnostics until "all things work together" (NLV).

He's also not afraid to get His hands dirty. Whatever mess you're in, He's in it with you. God is never disgusted, discouraged, disappointed, or disinterested. He has one aim, and that's to get you up and running.

. . . for the good . . . Romans 8:28

This is a key phrase. *Key.* "Everything that happens fits into a pattern for good" (Phillips) as God works "toward something good and beautiful" (VOICE) in our lives even if it doesn't appear so right this minute.

When you clean out a closet, you know how things look worse before they get better? Clothes piled here and there. Dust flying around the room. Boxes for Goodwill, for storage, for giveaway strewn across the floor. At some point you lose heart and think that you'll never be finished, that you'll live in this pigpen forever.

But when you're finally done and everything's sorted, that clean closet is a thing of beauty. You open the door several times a day just to admire the view.

That's how God works in our lives. Hands on. Cleaning, straightening, repairing, overhauling, taking apart, putting back together. We don't know how or when our lives got so messy, and at this point it doesn't matter. We just need help.

Because He loves us, God is more than willing—and supremely able—to turn our garbage into a platform for His glory. Does He do this for everyone on the planet? Only for those who lift the hoods of their run-down cars or throw open the doors of their messy closets and say, "Oh, Lord, I'm so glad You're here. Please come in and stay forever."

. . . of those who love him, . . . Romans 8:28

So, do you love God? I'm not talking about a warm, happy feeling. I'm talking about commitment and trust and sacrifice. No question, God loves you. I'm asking, do you love Him? Do you believe what He has for you is for your good? That's the real test of faith, isn't it? To say, "Yes, God, whatever You have for me in this life I will receive as a gift of love from Your hands."

When well-meaning people tell us, "God never gives you more than you can handle," they are not quoting Scripture. They aren't even speaking the truth. God intentionally gives us more than we can handle so we'll recognize He is the One who will handle things. All things. Everything.

Maybe they're misquoting the verse "God is faithful; he will not let you be tempted beyond what you can bear,"[1] which falls in the middle of Paul's teaching on idol worship and other sins. It is comforting to know that when temptation rears its ugly head, God will provide a means of escape. But nowhere does the Bible say we are to handle challenges on our own. It's always God providing the way out. God doing the heavy lifting.

When we're overwhelmed with grief, do we keep telling ourselves, *I can handle this*? No, we turn to God and say, "My soul is weary with sorrow; strengthen me according to your word."[2]

When we're ready to drop with exhaustion or we fear we're losing our way, do we insist, "I can handle this"? No, we repeat this truth: "It is God who arms me with strength and keeps my way secure."[3]

. . . who have been called . . . *Romans 8:28*

Not called on the phone. Not called to be missionaries or evangelists. Simply "called to be saints" (DRA). Members of God's family. One of "the people God chose, because that was his plan" (ERV). When you were "summoned" (OJB), you responded. When God reached out, you said yes by the power of His Holy Spirit and accepted "His invitation to live according to His plan" (VOICE).

. . . according to his purpose. *Romans 8:28*

His hands are hard at work shaping and molding us "in fulfilment of his design" (KNOX) and "in keeping with his purpose" (NIrV). "We are the clay, you are the potter; we are all the work of your hand."[4]

More messiness, more mystery. Will we become water jars or flower vases? Have two handles or none? Be glazed or plain?

His Word gently reminds us, "Does the clay say to the potter, 'What are you making?'"[5] Nope. I personally believe the pot says, "You are trustworthy, Lord. Whatever You are making, it is good." Because it is "purposeful" (OJB). And because someday we will be a finished work of art standing in His glorious presence.

Once we accept the truth that He is the King of kings and we are the queens of zip, life becomes more joyful, change becomes more manageable, pain becomes more bearable, hope becomes more certain, and love becomes more real.

Lord, I confess I've used this verse as a platitude,
as a quick bandage to cover someone's gaping wound.
Now I see it for what it really is:
Your sovereign will at work.
You doing what You do best.
You looking out for our good.
You being You.

His Word, Your Heart

Romans 8:28 from the New International Version:

And we know that in all things God works
for the good of those who love him,
who have been called according to his purpose.

Romans 8:28 from your favorite translation:

10

Charm School

Charm is deceptive, and beauty is fleeting;
but a woman who fears the LORD is to be praised.

PROVERBS 31:30

*B*ack in the day, young women went to charm school to learn all the social graces—how to sit, stand, and walk properly, how to dine in a formal setting, how to address people in all strata of society.

One skill that definitely wasn't taught was deception. Sadly, some of us learned how to do that by ourselves, with a little help from the Father of Lies.

Charm is deceptive, . . . *Proverbs 31:30*

Charm sounds like a good thing. The Hebrew word *chanan* means "favor, grace, elegance." However, when charm is used for the wrong reasons, those "pleasing ways lie" (NLV). The old saying "Flattery will get you everywhere"? That's the charm we're talking about, the kind used to "fool" (EXB) people for our own benefit.

A telemarketer called our home one evening, selling a long-distance service. She pressed on with a cheery, singsong rendition of the script that was obviously before her until Bill finally said, "Ma'am, I'm afraid I don't have time for this conversation."

Her friendly tone turned to steel. "We are not having a conversation, Mr. Higgs. I am telling you about my product."

So charming.

> . . . and beauty is fleeting; . . . *Proverbs 31:30*

American novelist Faith Baldwin said, "Time is a dressmaker specializing in alterations." We know that's right. Beauty as the world defines it doesn't hang around long. The firm muscle tone of youth "fades away" (cev) with each passing year, and wrinkle-free skin finally "disappears" (gnt) despite all the age-defying (or is it age-denying?) products on the market.

In Hebrew *hebel* shows us why beauty "can trick you" (ncv). The word literally means "vapor, breath." *Poof.* Gone. In the end attractiveness "comes to nothing" (nlv) and will "vanish" (cjb) without a trace.

Am I saying an older woman isn't beautiful? Absolutely not! Her silvery hair, a few permanent smile lines, the glow of wisdom in her eyes? All stunning. But the media would have us believe otherwise. Their message is "Looking good means looking young." When an older woman is trotted out? She's inevitably described as "youthful for her age." *Sigh.*

Our Proverbs 31 sister has a different way of doing things.

> . . . but a woman who fears the Lord . . . *Proverbs 31:30*

She's the kind of woman who lives "reverently and worshipfully" (ampc), who "honors the Lord" (cev) and shows Him the deepest "respect" (nirv).

Fear is the right word for it, considering His limitless power.

Fear God, and there's no need to fear anyone or anything else.

We've seen how gorgeous God's woman can be. Her eyes shine with His love, her mouth smiles with His joy, her hands move at His bidding, and her feet follow where He leads. She exudes His peace, she offers His hope, she knows His Word, she speaks His truth, she embraces His people, and she glorifies His name.

She's the woman we all want to be when we grow up.

God alone makes that possible. It isn't a matter of trying harder or doing more. It's simply knowing God is at the very center of our lives and entrusting each minute to His more-than-capable hands.

. . . is to be praised. Proverbs 31:30

Hmm. Is such a woman going to be praised by people? I wouldn't count on it. People withhold praise for lots of reasons—jealousy and envy among them. Yet this verse assures us a godly woman "deserves to be praised" (cev) and, in fact, "will be greatly praised" (nlt). By whom? Her hubby and kids, for starters: "Her children arise and call her blessed; her husband also, and he praises her."[1]

So how's this going at your house? How about at work? Among friends? The truth is, trying to please people—even people we love— might never earn us applause. That's okay. They are not our audience.

Singer and speaker Annie Chapman wisely said, "The balanced woman is not out to please some of the people all the time, or all of the people some of the time. . . . Her strategy for living is to be simply, purely, passionately devoted to the Lord."[2]

There's our answer: God is the One who will ultimately praise us.

The Hebrew word for *praise* here is *halal,* which means "shine." God turns the warmth of His light on us, He shines His attention on us, He bathes us in the glow of His approval—not because we're good, but because we belong to Him and He is good.

Job remembered "the days when God watched over me, when his

lamp shone on my head."[3] Those days returned for Job, and they can become a reality for you and for me. Not by polishing our personalities or buffing up our appearance, but by loving, serving, honoring, and worshiping the One who is worthy of our praise.

Heavenly Father, I've spent
too many years trying to be charming
so others would like me.
Too much effort trying to be pretty
so others would look at me.
Help me turn to You with holy fear and humble trust.
If applause comes my way, let it be from You.
If You shine Your favor on me,
may it be for Your glory alone.

His Word, Your Heart

> **Tip #10 for memorizing Scripture:**
> Say the verse aloud.
> The best way to make the words
> stick is to recite them.

Proverbs 31:30 from the New International Version:

Charm is deceptive,
and beauty is fleeting;
but a woman who fears the Lord
is to be praised.

Proverbs 31:30 from your favorite translation:

11

Just Stop

He says, "Be still, and know that I am God;
I will be exalted among the nations,
I will be exalted in the earth."

PSALM 46:10

Beloved by millions, this scripture was especially meaningful to Martin Luther. "When he heard any discouraging news, he would say, 'Come let us sing the forty-sixth psalm.'"[1]

Here's why this verse spoke to his heart and still speaks to ours.

He says, "Be still, . . ." *Psalm 46:10*

As soothing as those words may sound, God means them as a gentle but firm reproof. "Calm down" (CEV), He says, Father to child. "That's enough!" (CEB). God was speaking very pointedly to his battle-prone people. "Stop fighting" (ERV), "cease striving" (NASB), and "desist" (YLT).

Okay, then. It's clear we are to lay down our weapons and trust God for the victory that will certainly be His.

I can almost sense the weight of His hands on my shoulders. You too? Is He holding us back? Or pulling us closer? *Yes.* The Hebrew word *raphah* literally means "sink" or "relax." The Lord is asking us to rest in His embrace. And let go.

We nod in agreement even as we hang on to our many concerns with both hands. If we don't worry about our parents' health, who will? If we don't fret over our children's future, who will? If we don't agonize over life's disappointments, big and small, who will?

God will. That's what He wants us to understand.

"... and know ..." *Psalm 46:10*

Only when we stop striving and "take a long, loving look" (MSG) can we "recognize" (AMP) the truth about God. About His mighty power and His matchless strength. About His sovereignty, now and forever.

Only when we seek the mind of Christ can we "know" (ASV).

Only when we remain still can we "see" (VOICE).

Only when we admit we don't understand can we "learn" (CEV).

Have you ever said, "I know that I know that I know"? That's what we're talking about here. Absolute conviction. Unwavering certainty.

"... that I am God; ..." *Psalm 46:10*

Not just any god with a small *g*, but "the True God" (VOICE). In Hebrew *elohim* is a plural word. Father, Son, and Holy Spirit. The whole of God.

Elsewhere in His Word we're reminded "the LORD is God"[2] and "there is no other."[3] Look no further. Search no longer. Seek no more.

Be still. Believe.

One Thursday I was behind the wheel as my husband and I breezed along a narrow country road. All at once a car coming from the opposite direction swerved into our lane and headed straight toward us. The road had no shoulder, no passing lane, and no obvious way I could escape a head-on collision.

Three words pounded in my heart. *Be still. Know.*

With only a split second to act, I dived into the grassy embankment and steered around a telephone pole, a large electrical transformer, an enormous tree, and one very long fence. When I braked to a stop without hitting any of the above, I was amazingly calm. No tears, no trauma, no trembling hands.

Another car that had also been forced off the road pulled up behind us. "Are you okay?" the anxious driver wanted to know.

"Fine," we both assured her, blinking at each other in astonishment. We *were* fine. So was our car. Clearly, the Lord had spared us. While I was being still, He was steering.

The best part of sharing that story? Giving God the glory He deserves! *Whew.*

". . . I will be exalted among the nations, . . ." *Psalm 46:10*

This isn't followed by a disclaimer—*if* things turn out according to God's plans or *if* we don't destroy the planet first. No, it's going to happen. "All nations on earth will honor me" (CEV), God declares. He "will be praised in all the nations" (NCV) and "be exalted among the heathen" (GNV).

Wow. Even people who are looking in the wrong direction? Yes. "At the name of Jesus every knee should bow, in heaven and on earth and under the earth, and every tongue acknowledge that Jesus Christ is Lord, to the glory of God the Father."[4]

". . . I will be exalted in the earth." *Psalm 46:10*

If a person ever said such a thing, we would shrink back in disgust. What hubris! But this is God speaking, the One who stands "supreme"

(GNT) and "above everything" (MSG). He rightly claims, "I am exalted throughout the world!" (CEB).

Oh, Lord. "Who is like you—majestic in holiness, awesome in glory, working wonders?"[5] We know the answer. No one is like our God.

He made the smallest fern and the tallest mountain, the sheep in the pasture and the swans on the lake. He also made running streams, wispy clouds, and icy glaciers from the waters that cover the earth. "And God saw that it was good."[6]

Then the Lord created you. "And it was very good."[7] Do you believe that about yourself? Because God does. He knew what He was doing the day He made you, and He knows what He is doing now.

Lord, help me be still and not strive,
stand in place without stamping my foot,
trust in the promised victory,
and anticipate the day when
the whole world will know
You are God.

His Word, Your Heart

> **Tip #11 for memorizing Scripture:**
> Stand up and walk around to stay
> energized and focused.

Psalm 46:10 from the New International Version:

He says, "Be still,
and know that I am God;
I will be exalted among the nations,
I will be exalted in the earth."

Psalm 46:10 from your favorite translation:

12

Love Song

The LORD your God is with you,
the Mighty Warrior who saves.
He will take great delight in you;
in his love he will no longer rebuke you,
but will rejoice over you with singing.

ZEPHANIAH 3:17

This verse will steal your breath. It might even make you blush. Oh, the things God has in store for you, His beloved bride! Whenever the truth of God's love is yanked from our grasp by a culture that focuses on negativity and majors in cynicism, it's time to dive into His Word and be refreshed. *Ahhhh.*

The LORD your God is with you, . . . *Zephaniah 3:17*

This is everything we need to know: His name, His relationship with us, and the assurance of His presence. The God of the universe, the

One who claimed you long before you claimed Him, is "in your midst" (LEB). I'm telling you, He's "right there with you" (CJB).

Right. There.

Just because we can't see God, that doesn't make Him any less real. I'm gazing out my living room window at a stream of sunlight pouring across our lawn. His sky, His sun, His grass, His ground. All of creation points to our Creator. He is real, His works are tangible, and He is here.

He is "present among you" (MSG) all the time. "Living among you" (NLT), day in and day out. The Enemy will try to convince you that God has forgotten you, neglected you, abandoned you, and turned His back on you, but that's simply not possible. "The LORD your God is with you." If those were the only words in the Bible, they would be enough. But He gave us so much more.

. . . the Mighty Warrior who saves. *Zephaniah 3:17*

He's not idly standing around, this God of ours. He's fighting our battles. And He's winning. Our "powerful soldier" (ERV), our "champion" (VOICE), our "savior" (NLT) never grows weary, never lays down His weapons. Instead, He celebrates "victory after victory" (CEV) on our behalf.

When you feel defeated, exhausted, depleted, it's time to step back and give God room to wage war against your enemies, because His "power gives you victory" (GNT) and His "strength shall deliver thee" (KNOX).

Nowhere in the Bible are we told, "Save yourself." We couldn't possibly do it, try as we might. God alone rescues. God alone saves. Hold on tight, dear one, knowing He will never let go. Never.

He will take great delight in you; . . . *Zephaniah 3:17*

The imagery shifts from a strong, mighty warrior to a tender-hearted suitor. Matthew Henry wrote, "God not only loves his saints, but he loves to love them."[1] When you're deeply in love, you think of that special person around the clock. You cherish each moment you have together. Your loved one's face, voice, and smile brighten your day. No one matters more to you.

That's how God feels about you. Not because you are always lovable, but because He is always loving.

> . . . in his love he will no longer rebuke you, . . .
> *Zephaniah 3:17*

Okay, I'm just going to say it: I'm not crazy about this translation. Right in the middle of all this love-soaked language comes the sharp word *rebuke*. Most English translations don't go there. Instead, they promise He will "quiet you by his love" (ESV), or "create calm with his love" (CEB), or cause you to "rest in his love" (ASV).

The original Hebrew isn't much help, offering several different meanings for the verb *charash*. It all adds up to this: God will hold His peace. He will keep your faults to Himself rather than naming them one by one. "In His love He will be silent and make no mention [of past sins, or even recall them]" (AMPC).

That's some kind of love, sisters.

When I hold my tongue rather than scold my husband about leaving his dirty socks on the floor (again), that's love. In turn, if my husband doesn't say a word when a mail-order package arrives from my favorite online retailer (again), that's love. Small love next to God's love yet earthly proof that silence is golden.

Quietly, gently He will "calm all your fears" (NLT) and "give you new life" (NLV) and "show you his love once again" (WYC).

While those are amazing promises, this next bit puts me right over the top.

> . . . but will rejoice over you with singing. *Zephaniah 3:17*

God sings? Over us? Yes, He does.

It's not just a metaphor. There are notes involved. "He celebrates and sings because of you" (CEV) and will "delight you with his songs" (MSG). Clearly this is something the Lord enjoys doing, because He promises to "laugh and be happy" (ERV) as He lets loose "shouts of joy" (AMP).

Your worthiness, your goodness, your faithfulness aren't even mentioned here. God loves you because He chooses to. God loves you because it gives Him pleasure to do so. This verse assures us, "He celebrates and sings because of you, and he will refresh your life with his love" (CEV).

Be refreshed, my sister. His love for you makes all things new.

Lord, to think of You being close to me,
saving me, delighting in me,
loving me, accepting me,
rejoicing over me,
singing to me.
Oh!

His Word, Your Heart

Tip #12 for memorizing Scripture:

Use gestures with each word
to emphasize and illustrate the verse.

Zephaniah 3:17 from the New International Version:

The LORD your God is with you,
the Mighty Warrior who saves.
He will take great delight in you;
in his love he will no longer rebuke you,
but will rejoice over you with singing.

Zephaniah 3:17 from your favorite translation:

13

All Grown Up

Start children off on the way they should go,
and even when they are old they
will not turn from it.

Proverbs 22:6

*M*aybe you've seen this verse posted in a church nursery, urging parents to raise their little ones to walk the straight and narrow so they'll stick to that path when they're older.

But the women who cling to this verse for dear life aren't mothers of toddlers. No, they're mothers and grandmothers of teenagers or grown children who've lost their way. If that's you, sister, you have so much company. Don't lose heart. God is beside your loved one just as He is beside you, and He is not about to let go.

Even if you don't have kids or grandkids, God has a word waiting for you here, I promise.

Start children off . . . Proverbs 22:6

I'm partial to the King James Version's wording of this verse: "Train up a child." It's a spot-on translation of the Hebrew word *chanak,* meaning to "train up, dedicate," like fitting a rope halter to a horse.

Being the parent is the hardest part of parenting. Loving your kids? Easy. Caring for their daily needs? Intense but manageable. Carpooling them from A to B? Time-consuming but a great chance for meaningful conversation.

The challenges come when we must "teach" (CEV) our kids how to do life. That means learning how to "direct" (NLT) them without pushing or pulling. And how to "give instruction" (YLT) patiently instead of just barking out orders (*oops*).

Such efforts are day-in and day-out difficult but gotta-do-it necessary.

> . . . on the way they should go, . . . *Proverbs 22:6*

The Hebrew word *derek,* translated "way," also means "road, distance, journey, manner." We're called to teach our kids not only the right destination but also "the right path" (TLB), the one God calls "right and just and fair—every good path."[1]

What if they're stumbling or veering off in the wrong direction? Should we panic? Jesus said of His followers, "I give them eternal life, and they shall never perish; no one will snatch them out of my hand."[2]

No one. *No one.*

Now consider this. "They should go" is *peh* in Hebrew, which literally means "mouth." We're back to the horse that's unhappy about the halter knotted around his head, like a kid who balks at being asked to follow the house rules.

An untamed horse is beautiful to look at but of little use to its owner—until a horse trainer steps in. The trainer understands what's needed. He or she gently but firmly breaks the horse and then trains it according to the animal's natural strengths and abilities.

Along the same lines we're to train up our children "in a way that fits their needs" (ERV), always taking into account their "individual gift or bent" (AMPC), looking to God to guide us as we guide them.

For parents the word *trust* takes on a whole new meaning.

. . . and even when they are old . . . *Proverbs 22:6*

Old doesn't mean elderly here. It just means no longer a child. Old enough to make decisions without parental prompting. Old enough to be considered "grown" (CEV). This doesn't mean one particular birthday but "all their life" (GNT).

You never stop being a parent, right? God doesn't either. If your children placed their faith in Christ, you can be certain His hand will remain on their shoulders long after you've gone to glory.

. . . they will not turn from it. *Proverbs 22:6*

The Lord knew the desperately crooked path I would take when I turned seventeen. He walked beside me, rescued me daily, kept me alive. If He can save a wretch like me, I'm convinced He can save anyone.

Even if you didn't raise your children to know the Lord, even if you messed up a hundred times, God never messes up. "The Lord knows those who are his,"[3] and He will make certain they get home.

In the meantime keep loving them. Keep praying for them. Reach out to them even if they don't respond. Trust God to honor His wonderful promise: "Surely the arm of the LORD is not too short to save."[4] His arm is not too short to guide either.

Waiting to board a plane for home, I saw a handsome young man chat at length with an elderly woman in a wheelchair and then say to a nearby flight attendant, "May I escort my new friend to her seat?"

"Sorry. I'll need to do that," the attendant explained and then pointed the wheelchair toward the Jetway.

Clearly disappointed, he watched the older woman head for the plane. "Good talking to you, ma'am!" he called out. A moment later he reclaimed his seat and said to no one in particular, "Some people are just so nice."

"Like you," two people responded in unison. Smiles were exchanged, and a warm glow settled on those who were close enough to witness the uncommon scene. In the South we would say his mama raised him right. But the kindness in his eyes, in his speech, in his demeanor bore the mark of more training than even the most watchful mother could provide. It seemed his heavenly Father had done a fine job as well.

Lord, You are the only Parent
who gets everything right.
More than once
my parents were disappointed in me,
and I have failed my children
in so many ways.
Help me continue to train and teach them
to be wholly dependent on You.
Give me the courage to wait and trust,
knowing Your children are safely in Your hands.

His Word, Your Heart

Tip #13 for memorizing Scripture:
Record the verse on your phone
or a digital recorder.

Proverbs 22:6 from the New International Version:

Start children off
on the way they should go,
and even when they are old
they will not turn from it.

Proverbs 22:6 from your favorite translation:

14

Comfort Food

So do not fear, for I am with you;
do not be dismayed, for I am your God.
I will strengthen you and help you;
I will uphold you with my righteous right hand.

Isaiah 41:10

After a week of nonstop traveling and eating restaurant food, my daughter and I were ready for the plainest meal on the menu. No heavy sauces, no fancy side dishes, and definitely no fried foods.

The mixed grill turned out to be the ideal choice. Healthy portions of nothing but lean, boneless meat—steak, pork, lamb, and chicken—grilled to perfection. (If you're a vegetarian, how about a plate of grilled eggplant, asparagus, tomatoes, peppers, and zucchini?)

This verse is like that meal. Simple, straightforward nutrition that fills our hearts with everything we hunger for.

So . . . *Isaiah 41:10*

So. A small word that speaks volumes. It tells us, "Because the previous thing is true, then this is true." In the verse before this one in Isaiah, God promises His people, "I have chosen you and have not rejected you."[1] Since we are loved by God and chosen by God, we can trust what He says next.

. . . do not fear, . . . *Isaiah 41:10*

Calming words, comforting words. "Don't worry" (ERV), the Lord says. "Don't panic" (MSG).

If I seem fairly confident to you, let me squash that misconception right now. I have a deep-seated fear that I constantly battle: claustrophobia. Tight, enclosed spaces really undo me. Window seats on airplanes? Low-ceilinged tunnels? Crowded elevators? A subway car packed with commuters? *Help.*

Your fears may take you down a different path. Whether we have a dread of spiders or snakes, heights or crowds, dogs or germs, our phobias are real, and so is the anxiety they produce.

Faced with an unsettling situation I can't avoid, I take long, deep breaths and cling to these words: "there is nothing to fear" (AMPC). God explains how that's possible.

. . . for I am with you; . . . *Isaiah 41:10*

That reality is what gets me through. I fix my eyes on my watch, reminding myself this ordeal won't last forever. Then I listen for God's silent assurance: "I am here, with you" (VOICE).

He is with you as well, beloved. Wherever you are and whatever you are doing, He's *on* your side and *by* your side. What a balm to our anxious hearts to know we are never alone.

. . . do not be dismayed, . . . *Isaiah 41:10*

The Hebrew word *shaah* means "to gaze," which is why some translations tell us "do not look around" (AMPC) or "turn not aside" (DRA). But that's exactly what we do when we're afraid. We lose sight of the One in charge. We forget we have a God who cares. That's why He gently encourages us, "Do not anxiously look about you" (NASB) and "let nothing terrify you!" (GNT).

Where we aim our gaze really matters. Are we looking for someone or something to rescue us? Or are we looking to our Savior, who has already done so?

> . . . for I am your God. *Isaiah 41:10*

He is not only with us. He is also in charge of us. He is our Creator, our Redeemer, our King. When He asks, "Am I not thy God?" (KNOX), we have the chance to say again, "Yes, Lord. You are."

Committing our lives to God isn't a one-time event. It's an ongoing experience. Every time we see some variation of "I am your God" in Scripture, that's our cue to embrace the truth and respond in kind, "I am Your child."

Even if your earthly parents dropped the ball, you can be very sure God did not, cannot, and will not. He is the Father you can trust completely.

> I will strengthen you and help you; . . . *Isaiah 41:10*

Our culture encourages us to be self-sufficient. But Paul spoke the truth: "when I am weak, then I am strong."[2] Walking in faith doesn't mean we never stumble. It means we humbly accept God's help so we can stand.

I've heard people say, "Christianity is for the weak." Exactly. Admitting our weakness is how we discover God's strength.

... I will uphold you with my righteous right hand.
Isaiah 41:10

There it is: that mighty strength will "retain you" (AMPC), "support you" (CJB), and "hold you steady" (MSG). Like a soaring eagle, God lifts us high above the fears and concerns that try to drag us down.

God promises He will "keep a firm grip on you" (MSG) with His *righteous* right hand. What's that about? It's the hand of deliverance: "Your right hand, LORD, shattered the enemy."[3] It's the hand of blessing: "You will fill me with joy in your presence, with eternal pleasures at your right hand."[4] And it's the hand of power: "Your hand is strong, your right hand exalted."[5]

That's the hand clasping yours. Not yanking you around like an impatient baby-sitter or squeezing too hard like a bully at school. This is the hand of the One who cherishes you. His grip is firm yet loving. And He never lets go.

"I am," He says twice. "I will," He says twice. Delicious and satisfying, His assurances are comfort food for the soul.

Oh, Lord,
I am more fearful
than I want to be
and more easily undone
than I should be.
Help me place my hand in Yours
knowing You will hold on tight.

His Word, Your Heart

> **Tip #14 for memorizing Scripture:**
> Write the verse across a sheet of paper.
> Some of us learn best by speaking words,
> others by writing them.

Isaiah 41:10 from the New International Version:

So do not fear, for I am with you;
do not be dismayed, for I am your God.
I will strengthen you and help you;
I will uphold you with my righteous right hand.

Isaiah 41:10 from your favorite translation:

15

Fret Not

Do not be anxious about anything,
but in every situation,
by prayer and petition, with thanksgiving,
present your requests to God.

PHILIPPIANS 4:6

"Fear not"? Right. Got that. Now it's time for something harder: "Fret not."

Sister, I'm a world-class worrier. I worry about not finishing a project on time. Then I worry no one will like it. If they do like it, I worry they won't like the next one.

Been there? There now? Then this verse is definitely for you. Even if you've heard it a hundred times, let's see if we can find, tucked between the lines, a fresh truth that will unlock the secret of how to stop fretting.

Do not be anxious . . . *Philippians 4:6*

It reads like a command. "Do not fret" (AMPC). "Never worry" (ISV). Already I'm in trouble because (big surprise) I don't like someone telling me what to do. The best bosses I ever had were the ones who told me what they wanted yet made me think it was my idea.

God follows an entirely different management model. When He asks us to do something, He clearly states that it's entirely His idea, and then He gives us sufficient strength to carry out His plan. That's why we don't need to fret.

... about anything, ... *Philippians 4:6*

God doesn't want one thing left on our stuff-to-worry-about list. "Nothing must make you anxious" (KNOX), He says. And that Greek word *médeis* means "not even one."

What's the biggest concern in your life right now? The huge thing pressing on your heart 24/7? God says not to worry about that.

Nope. Not even that.

... but ... *Philippians 4:6*

"But" sounds pretty negative, yet it's simply pointing us to the alternative to worrying, fretting, and being anxious. "Instead" (NET), "rather" (CEB), "on the contrary" (CJB), here's what happens when we go with God's plan even in the midst of life's challenges.

... in every situation, ... *Philippians 4:6*

Every is one of those words you can't get around. Not *some,* not *most.* "Every circumstance" (AMP), the Lord assures us. "Every need" (KNOX). However long our tally of concerns extends, God is already there.

A prodigal child? An alcoholic spouse? An empty bank account? A troubling lab report? A layoff at work? An ailing parent? Yes, all those situations. Hard, hard, hard but not too hard for God.

Also, nothing is too simple for God's notice. He understands the small things that are big to us. He knows and cares and wants to hear about them.

. . . by prayer . . . *Philippians 4:6*

In the Greek, *proseuché* means interactive prayer. Not just talking, but also listening and waiting for the Lord's response. No need to worry about saying just the right words in just the right way, because "the Spirit helps us in our weakness. We do not know what we ought to pray for, but the Spirit himself intercedes for us."[1]

In my childhood when my brothers and sisters gathered around the dinner table, I was the one who prayed before the meal. Not because I knew the Lord, but because I was the youngest and knew a simple prayer that began "God is great, God is good." Even though I didn't fully understand His goodness, I spoke the truth of it, scattering seeds across the soil of my heart. When we pray, God hears, and we hear the truth as well.

. . . and petition, . . . *Philippians 4:6*

This sounds like a legal term: "Here, sign a petition." What it really means is seeking, asking, entreating, "beseeching" (KNOX). To put it simply, "ask and pray" (NIrV). Rather than fretting and fussing, "shape your worries into prayers" (MSG).

Now, here's the hidden key that sets us free.

. . . with thanksgiving, . . . *Philippians 4:6*

Even while we're asking and praying, we're already thanking God for listening and answering. We're also thanking Him for "all he has done"

(NLT) in the past, all He is doing right now, and all He is going to do in the future.

Gratitude takes faith, my sister. Faith is the opposite of fretfulness. It enables us to pray "with a thankful heart" (GNT). A trusting heart. A believing heart.

If you're looking for something meaningful to write in your journal today, this sums up our lesson from the Lord: "Do not worry about anything. Talk to God about everything. Thank him for what you have. Ask him for what you need" (WE).

. . . present your requests to God. *Philippians 4:6*

It's also translated "ask" (NCV) and "tell" (NIrV), but the verb "present" helps us imagine handing the Lord our needs like gifts, neatly boxed and wrapped in ribbons. You and I know how it works with gifts. Once they're placed in someone else's hands, we can't take them back.

No matter how ugly those worries look to you, God will gladly take care of them. "He longs to hear your requests" (VOICE), so don't hesitate to tell Him everything. "Make your wants known to God" (AMPC). Yes, "every detail of your needs" (Phillips). Your concerns are not a burden to Him. They are not a nuisance. They are beautiful gifts of faith and trust and gratitude. *My needs are all Yours, Lord. Thank You for taking them.*

Some translations end this verse with a semicolon or a comma, meaning there's more good news to come in the next verse. I'm including those encouraging words here so we can celebrate the happy ending: "And the peace of God, which transcends all understanding, will guard your hearts and your minds in Christ Jesus."[2]

Fret not, my friend.

Heavenly Father,
You've shown me what I need to do.
Now help me do it.
Gently prod me when I start to worry.
Prompt me to pray.
Urge me to listen.
Remind me to be grateful.
Always, ever grateful.

His Word, Your Heart

> **Tip #15 for memorizing Scripture:**
> Once you've written the verse,
> underline or highlight the key words.

Philippians 4:6 from the New International Version:

Do not be anxious about anything,
but in every situation,
by prayer and petition, with thanksgiving,
present your requests to God.

Philippians 4:6 from your favorite translation:

King Jams supplication vs petition
Careful vs Anxious
Good news

Dont worry about Anything, but in
all your prayers ask God for what
you need, with a Thankful heart
always asking him

16

It's Tough to Be Gentle

A gentle answer turns away wrath,
but a harsh word stirs up anger.

PROVERBS 15:1

When common sense is no longer common, we need God's wisdom more than ever.

Consider this verse from Proverbs. It sounds easy, the kind of thing everybody knows how to do. A righteous anger-management plan. But knowing what's right and actually doing it? That's where wisdom comes in. And having the strength to do it? That's where God comes in.

A gentle answer . . . *Proverbs 15:1*

When someone is being nice, it's easy to respond in a way that's "soft" (ASV) and "sensitive" (CEB) and "mild" (DRA). That's not the situation in this verse. The other person isn't being remotely "tender" (EXB) or "kind" (CEV). He or she is full of wrath. Downright cruel. Lashing out.

At this point we have a choice. Either we can defuse the situation, or we can make it explode.

> ... turns away wrath, ... *Proverbs 15:1*

Amid the "fury" (CJB) that's flying around the room, the "anger" (EXB) that's heating the air, the "rage" (VOICE) that makes us want to strike back, the Holy Spirit surprises us.

Give them the last thing they deserve or expect. Give them mercy, kindness, and love.

Oh my. It's so hard to behave contrary to our feelings. Yet look what happens when we do. The Hebrew word *shub* means "to turn back." In essence, to repent. To turn around, to go back to God. When we respond to anger with kindness, we show people how much God loves them and how deep His mercy flows.

That's why His Word urges us, "As God's chosen people, holy and dearly loved, clothe yourselves with compassion, kindness, humility, gentleness and patience."[1] The Lord knows that gentleness "deflects" (CJB) negativity and then "diverts" (ISV) it in another direction. A genuine word of compassion "soothes" (CEV) ruffled feathers and "makes anger disappear" (ERV).

Back in my Bad Girl days, I marched into the radio sales office one Friday waving a fistful of commercials I was expected to record even though my workday was over. I'll spare you the ugly diatribe, but one coworker's response is worth repeating. A gentle-spirited believer, she had tears in her eyes when she said, "Liz, I love you, but I can't bear when you act like this."

The cup of cool water she poured on my hot temper doused the fire instantly. Especially her words of affection, something I'd not heard in years: "Liz, I love you." I was undone. I was also one step closer to embracing the God who loved my friend and (she assured me repeatedly) loved me too.

What an amazing truth. What an amazing Savior!

. . . but . . . Proverbs 15:1

Yes, *but.* This is what happens when we're guided by our flawed human nature rather than God's wisdom. We know in our hearts and minds what we should do, but we follow our raw feelings instead.

A vague memory of God's command to turn the other cheek[2] may flit through our minds, but we're too hurt or embarrassed or red faced or hotheaded to consider why the Lord might ask us to do such a difficult thing.

In the heat of the moment, we don't act; we react.

We fight fire with fire. We strike back.

. . . a harsh word . . . Proverbs 15:1

Our words are "sharp" (EXB) like a knife, "rough" (ERV) on the ego, and "grievous" (ASV) to the heart. We are "offensive" (CEB) by choice and are "mean" (NIrV) by intent. The "hard" (WYC) words we speak are designed to inflict maximum pain. We may call it self-defense—"Hey, she started it!"—but our response doesn't demonstrate our faith in a grace-giving God.

After that, things quickly go downhill.

. . . stirs up anger. Proverbs 15:1

That other person? Now she's really mad. "Tempers rise" (CJB) in tandem, and "fury" (DRA) escalates. Our heart rates go up, our blood pressure increases, and our bodies produce more testosterone. That leads to "more anger" (NCV) and a strong desire for "vengeance" (WYC).

This Hebrew word *aph* not only means "anger." It's also the word for "nostril, nose, face." We literally get in each other's face, nostrils flaring. This anger isn't only on the inside; it's very much on display, and it's ugly. We may not hit each other, but we will definitely hurt each other, often inflicting painful wounds that fester and refuse to heal.

Is the problem the other person's anger? No. The problem is our own pride. The pride that won't bow to God's leading. The pride that's determined to win battles rather than win souls.

As I write this, my heart is heavy. How many times have I used a sharp retort, focusing on retaliation instead of reconciliation? How many hours have I wasted grinding my teeth when I could have humbly submitted to the Spirit's leading and watched a miracle take place—a relationship restored, a prisoner set free?

In my heart I long to be gentle. In my day-to-day life, I have a long way to go.

My sister, if you struggle with a short fuse, remember that Christ's love is "wide and long and high and deep."[3] He is already preparing your heart for the next time someone jumps in your face so you can respond with His mercy, His kindness, His compassion, and His love.

Lord Jesus.
Help me trust in the strength
and power of the Holy Spirit
to guard my tongue and guide my actions.
Help me think beyond the present outrage
to the possibility of a positive outcome.
Help me resist what comes naturally
and by Your power do what comes
supernaturally.

His Word, Your Heart

Tip #16 for memorizing Scripture:
Write and rewrite the verse
as many times as you can fit it
on a sheet of paper.

Proverbs 15:1 from the New International Version:
A gentle answer turns away wrath,
but a harsh word stirs up anger.

Proverbs 15:1 from your favorite translation:

17

This Is It

Give thanks <u>in all</u> circumstances;
for this is God's will for you in Christ Jesus.

1 THESSALONIANS 5:18

not for all.

E ver longed to know God's will for your life? This is it. Two words: *give thanks.*

If you're thinking God's will for your life is unique and personalized and not like anyone else's, that's just not how it works, beloved. His will is the same for everyone: *give thanks.* How you manage that, what shape and form your gratitude takes—that's what makes these two words truly yours, as individual as your thumbprint.

Give thanks . . . *1 Thessalonians 5:18*

Not just on the fourth Thursday in November but all year long "always be thankful" (ERV) and "keep thanking God" (CEV). As the pilgrims might have said, "Do ye thankings" (WYC).

By God's design humility goes hand in hand with gratitude. Both require us to surrender any "I've got this" kind of thinking or a "Thanks but no thanks" attitude. Instead, we need to simply say yes. Yes to our neediness. Yes to our brokenness. Yes to God. And yes—always yes—to gratitude.

"Thank You." Really that's it. In word and in spirit.

The next bit is what makes giving thanks challenging.

. . . in all circumstances; . . . *1 Thessalonians 5:18*

Wait. God is asking us to be grateful "in every situation" (CEB), "no matter what the circumstances may be" (AMPC)? Oh boy. You and I both can think of situations in which it would be nearly impossible to say "Thank You."

Ann Voskamp's bestseller *One Thousand Gifts* is about living a life of gratitude, seeing everything as a gift from God's hand. To be honest, some days it's easier to count all the things that went wrong than to add up all the things that went right. That's why we need to count both and then give thanks for the good times *and* the bad times, knowing "God has made the one as well as the other."[1]

. . . for this is God's will for you . . . *1 Thessalonians 5:18*

Make no mistake. "This is what God wants you to do" (CEV), and "this is how God wants you to live" (ERV). In the process "you will be working out the will of God" (Phillips).

Since we can't actually *see* His will, can we trust that it's good? You bet. Fact is, we trust what we can't see every day of our lives.

Let's say you order a pizza over the phone. When you hang up, you trust them to make your pizza, right? You don't call back every five minutes and say, "Are you making it? Are you sure?" You believe. You trust.

You *know* they are making your pizza. You're so certain of it you get in your car and drive there to pick it up and aren't the least bit surprised when they pull it out of the oven, fresh and hot.

Why do you have so much faith in the pizza place? Because the last twenty times you called, that's how it worked. (Okay, there was one time they accidentally gave your pizza to somebody else, but you still trusted them enough to order another one a week later.)

Time after time they have proved themselves trustworthy, yes? Well, if you can trust the strangers who make your pizza, you can surely trust the One who made the sun, moon, and stars. God has proven His faithfulness over and over. Not twenty times. Not twenty thousand times. You can't actually put a number on it because "He is faithful in all he does."[2]

We see this guarantee in the One who claimed us as His own.

. . . in Christ Jesus. *1 Thessalonians 5:18*

Only those who belong to God's Son, who are "united with the Messiah" (CJB) and have His Spirit working inside them, can walk according to God's will.

The deepest joys, the richest prayer life, the most heartfelt thanks are possible because we aren't depending on our own strength, exerting our own wills. It's God's strength working in us and through us.

Now and again He reminds us of that.

One January I had a speaking engagement in eastern Pennsylvania. By the time the plane landed, I was in trouble. My ears were closed, my throat was swollen, and I was blowing my nose every two minutes. Oh, lovely.

When we reached the church, I wasn't entirely sure I could speak my name, let alone deliver three messages. My prayer was short and to the point. *Please, Lord. Please.*

God was already on it. The sanctuary had great acoustics, the microphone was up to snuff (okay, *sniff*), and the women in the audience were genuinely excited about being there.

Still, only the Lord could get me through this. I didn't just lean on Him. I clung to Him.

"Good morning," I began, relieved to hear more than a croak come out. A second sentence followed, then a third one. I was utterly aware of His Presence strengthening me, healing me, if only for those few necessary hours. I would say the wonder of it stole my breath, except I was breathing. Normally, naturally. My voice was strong, yet my knees were weak with joy.

By day's end I decided I should arrive at every speaking engagement on the verge of pneumonia just to watch God do what only He can do.

Thank You, thank You, thank You, Father.

I realize this story is trifling compared to the major challenges you may be facing right now. Here's the thing: if God is willing to strengthen us in the small, everyday, blow-your-nose moments, imagine what He can do in the midst of huge, life-changing, world-shaking situations.

While we wait for Him to move on our behalf, His will is clear: "Let the peace of Christ rule in your hearts. . . . And be thankful."[3]

Lord, I see now
that You aren't asking me to feel thankful.
You are asking me to be thankful.
To speak my gratitude aloud.
To say "Thank You" and truly mean it.

His Word, Your Heart

Tip #17 for memorizing Scripture:
Draw a picture to illustrate
the verse you're memorizing.

1 Thessalonians 5:18 from the New International Version:
Give thanks in all circumstances;
for this is God's will for you in Christ Jesus.

1 Thessalonians 5:18 from your favorite translation:

18

Lovely Thoughts

Finally, brothers and sisters,
whatever is true, whatever is noble,
whatever is right, whatever is pure,
whatever is lovely, whatever is admirable—
if anything is excellent or praiseworthy—
think about such things.

PHILIPPIANS 4:8

"Please forgive me." I've said this so often lately that I considered having it printed on a T-shirt just to save time.

Wait. I could have several shirts made, one for every occasion.

- Please forgive me for being pushy.
- Please forgive me for being late.
- Please forgive me for being busy.
- Please forgive me for being me.

That's the starter set, of course. The list of things I've done wrong is so long those please-forgive-me T-shirts could fill a Hollywood walk-in closet.

And I'm not talking about my before-I-knew-the-Lord years with all those flashy, splashy sins. Oh no. I'm talking about this week, with promises I've forgotten, deadlines I've missed, unkind words I wish I'd never said, and thoughts that don't qualify as true, noble, right, pure, lovely, admirable, excellent, or even remotely praiseworthy.

For Former Bad Girls this verse can be even more challenging. Ugly words and sordid images may linger in our minds for ten, twenty, thirty years after the fact—taunting us, shaming us, belittling us. My prayer is that God will use Philippians 4:8 to renew our minds and refill our hearts so completely that words like *pure* and *noble* make us feel clean instead of unworthy.

Finally, . . . Philippians 4:8

Everyone's favorite part of a long speech is "in conclusion" (CJB). But Paul's letter to the Philippians was so powerful, so joyful, the young church must have been sad when he neared the end. He offered this final call to a life of obedience, showing believers how we can walk forward with Christ "from now on" (CEB) and "for the rest" (DRA) of our lives.

. . . brothers and sisters, . . . Philippians 4:8

In Greek, *adelphoi* refers to all who are part of God's family. "My friends" (CEV) strikes an even more endearing note, and "beloved" (NRSV) is perfect.

The following virtues aren't meant to be a checklist—"Do this, and you're in." Instead, they point us in the right direction and get us thinking in new ways. God has spun these words out of pure gold, meant to dazzle the mind's eye.

. . . whatever is true, . . . Philippians 4:8

The first place to turn for truth? His timeless, matchless Word. The psalmist wrote, "All your words are true; all your righteous laws are eternal."[1] The *words* are what make the Bible sacred, not the paper and binding. Still, I'm not about to toss my Bible on the floor as if it's just any old book. Not this girl. Not in this lifetime.

. . . whatever is noble, . . . Philippians 4:8

The repetition of "whatever" is unusual—six times in one verse. It sets off and emphasizes each thing we're to think about. It also makes this passage read like poetry, each word chosen with special care.

As for "noble," the literal meaning is "venerable, grave," which is rather somber. I'm sticking with "noble." Maybe "honorable" (ASV). How about "seemly" (AMPC) or "honest" (KJV) or "respected" (NLV)? All are fine translations of a word that brings to mind something high and lifted up, like the Lord Himself.

Though He was counted among commoners at birth, Jesus is noble in every possible sense. Just as we look to God's Word for what is true, we can turn to His Son for what is noble.

. . . whatever is right, . . . Philippians 4:8

Right has nothing to do with politics and everything to do with ethics. We're to focus our minds on things that are "just" (RSV) and "reputable" (MSG) and "fair" (ISV), things that God would approve, that God would call "righteous" (CJB). So much for "Hey, nobody knows what's in my head!" God knows precisely what's in there. Every word, every image, every emotion. All of it.

Considering some of the stuff that wanders through my mind, I need a long, daily soak in a bath of grace. How comforting to know God is willing to wash us clean, again and again.

... whatever is pure, ... *Philippians 4:8*

The actress Tallulah Bankhead once said she was "pure as the driven slush."[2] Unfortunately, I get that. *Pure* is one of those words that pushes me back a step. How pure should we be? Ready for worship. Ready to stand before God.

Don't despair, friend. Don't think, *I can't possibly be that pure!* God promises to "purify us from all unrighteousness."[3] This holy business is all His. Our part is to *think* on all these good things. Fix our gaze on them. Make a habit of meditating on them.

... whatever is lovely, ... *Philippians 4:8*

Don't you love the word *lovely*? The Greek word *prosphilés* means "agreeable" and "dearly prized," like visiting a botanic garden with row after row of colorful blooms, each one more photogenic than the last.

Lovely is how we describe something that so fills our hearts with joy there's no room for sorrow or regret. Something "beautiful" (ERV) and "pleasing" (LEB), a balm for our souls and a respite for our minds.

... whatever is admirable— ... *Philippians 4:8*

God wants us to dwell on things that are "kind and winsome and gracious" (AMPC) so we might become like them. In a world where cynicism has replaced witticism, and being cruel to others, especially online, is par for the course, God is saying, "You can do better than that. You can be kinder than that."

... if anything is excellent or praiseworthy—
... *Philippians 4:8*

We sense Paul winding up things here. "Don't ever stop thinking about what is truly worthwhile" (cev), he said, "if you value the approval of God" (Phillips). For those of us who struggle with wanting the approval of people, this verse has the power to transform us completely. We're called to seek His approval and only His. Directing our thoughts toward things that please Him is the first step.

. . . think about such things. *Philippians 4:8*

If you're as weary as I am of engaging in a mental tug of war with your evil twin, who insists on cluttering your head with words and images that are anything but good, the Lord offers a simple but profound solution. "Weigh and take account of these things" (ampc), and "be made new in the attitude of your minds."[4]

Whatever ugliness the world throws at you today, this verse provides the antidote you need to fix your thoughts on all that's beautiful.

Heavenly Father,
because of Your endless patience and mercy,
I am learning to look in the right direction,
which helps me think in the right direction,
which helps me walk in the right direction.
The loveliest thing I gaze upon, Lord, is You.

His Word, Your Heart

Tip #18 for memorizing Scripture:
Try journaling while
you study God's Word.

Philippians 4:8 from the New International Version:

Finally, brothers and sisters,
whatever is true, whatever is noble,
whatever is right, whatever is pure,
whatever is lovely, whatever is admirable—
if anything is excellent or praiseworthy—
think about such things.

Philippians 4:8 from your favorite translation:

In conclusion my friends, fill your
minds with those things that are good
and that deserve praise, things that are
true, noble, right, pure, lovely and honorable.

19

Laughing Matters

She is clothed with strength and dignity;
she can laugh at the days to come.

PROVERBS 31:25

A verse with the word *laugh*? Yes, please.

The excellent woman described in Proverbs 31 certainly figured out the value of laughter. That's how she remained carefree, even with everything she had on her plate.

She is clothed . . . *Proverbs 31:25*

It's often the first thing we notice about a woman—her "clothing" (esv), "her garments" (isv). Our Proverbs 31 sister may be dressed for success, but she's not dressed for battle.

Fresh out of college my friends and I wore business attire as if it were a suit of armor when we headed out to slay the dragons of the corporate world. Case in point. In the deep recesses of my desk, I found a pad of sticky notes from the eighties, featuring a career woman's checklist for success: "Look like a lady. Act like a man. Work like a dog."

We've since learned it's who we are rather than what we wear that leads to genuine success. And it's what we do for others that truly matters in the end. As author Kate Halverson famously said, "If you are all wrapped up in yourself, you are overdressed."

. . . with strength . . . *Proverbs 31:25*

This Proverbs woman knew what to wear. She not only wore her own fabulous handmade creations, but she also wore strength and dignity like a shield, "as if they were her clothes" (NIrv).

The Hebrew word *oz* means "strength, might." This doesn't suggest we're to be strong willed to the point of stubbornness. Just the opposite. Strong enough to be flexible, without fear of losing control, knowing our "position is strong and secure" (AMP). It's the strength of the Lord that empowers us. "The LORD is my strength and my shield; my heart trusts in him, and he helps me."[1]

If Nehemiah 8:10—"the joy of the LORD is your strength"—is a source of encouragement to you, here's the rest of the story on that verse. After God's people were exiled in Babylon, they returned to Jerusalem and celebrated with a feast not unlike our Thanksgiving. Nehemiah said, "Go and enjoy choice food and sweet drinks, and send some to those who have nothing prepared. This day is holy to our Lord. Do not grieve, for the joy of the LORD is your strength."

Again we find strength and joy in a single verse. God's mighty power walks side by side with His mighty joy.

. . . and dignity; . . . *Proverbs 31:25*

How would you describe dignity? I'd say it's more about demeanor than social class. The Hebrew word *hadar* tells us this woman was dressed in "honor, splendor, majesty." Some translations go with "glory" (JUB) or "respect" (ERV).

Put them all together, and you get a sense of what God is calling His daughters to step into: His righteousness. His holiness. Impossible? Not when it's His doing. "I the LORD am holy—I who make you holy."[2] We're never too old—or too young—to walk in His strength and His splendor.

. . . she can laugh . . . Proverbs 31:25

Imagine being "full of joy" (NLV), someone who's "confident" (CEB) and "cheerful" (CEV), who's not "afraid" (GNT) or "anxious" (EXB). Why merely giggle when you could guffaw? Why simply smile when you can snort?

When I was growing up, my role models were funny women. First I loved Lucy. And Ethel. Then I longed to be Carol Burnett. Or Phyllis Diller, who said, "A smile is a curve that sets everything straight." My list of favorites grew, from Lily Tomlin to Gilda Radner, Madeline Kahn to Tina Fey, proving that women and humor make a fine duo.

Laughing is one way we express our true selves. We may learn how to walk, stand, sit, and eat properly, but when we genuinely laugh, we lay all pretense aside as our carefully polished image goes right out the window. That could be why my grown children like to take me to funny movies, since I invariably honk, howl, or hoot.

Laughter is good for our hearts, souls, and minds. It's a free gift from the Lord. No cost, no calories, no guilt. As comedian Fred Allen said, "It's bad to suppress laughter. It goes back down and spreads to your hips."

Sadly, humor isn't always welcome among God's people. One of my early books received a one-star review with the comment "She is just too silly for a mature Christian!" My heart sank when I read those words until the Lord reminded me that laughter and joy were His idea: "He will yet fill your mouth with laughter and your lips with shouts of joy."[3]

So I'm going with His plan.

. . . at the days to come. Proverbs 31:25

A woman of God not only laughs in the here and now; she also "smiles at the future" (NASB) and does so "without fear" (NLT). She's not overly concerned about her children, not frightened about her finances, not freaked out about getting older. She knows that "she and her family are in readiness for it" (AMPC) because their lives are grounded in God's truth and wrapped in His love.

When God laughs over His people, the sound is as gentle as His embrace. We may not *hear* His laughter, but we can sense His pleasure. We won't find *LOL* in His Word, but we do find the promise "so will your God rejoice over you."[4] He's also there to help us when we lose our sense of humor.

As a little kid, I was famous for stamping my foot whenever I threw a full-blown temper tantrum. My older siblings seldom hid their amusement. "Don't laugh at me!" I would fume, looking and sounding even more ridiculous. My brother Tom invariably found a way to make me giggle, then gave me a hug to ease my embarrassment.

God handles us in much the same way, helping us see how truly foolish we can be even as He shows us the depth of His joy in calling us His own.

With the Lord holding eternity in His hands, we can look "forward to the future with joy" (NCV). And laughter. And, yes, outright silliness.

Lord, I'm not only laughing at the future;
I'm having a blast in the present.
Help me resist the stern advice of others
to straighten up, to settle down, to get serious.
Let me hear Your gentle laughter
and receive it as a gift of love.

His Word, Your Heart

> **Tip #19 for memorizing Scripture:**
> Find a photo that suits the verse,
> creating another way to jog your memory.

Proverbs 31:25 from the New International Version:
She is clothed with strength and dignity;
she can laugh at the days to come.

Proverbs 31:25 from your favorite translation:

She is strong and respected and
not afraid of the future

Strength and self respect.

20

High Flying

But those who hope in the LORD
will renew their strength.
They will soar on wings like eagles;
they will run and not grow weary,
they will walk and not be faint.

ISAIAH 40:31

The Lord clearly has a sense of humor. I began writing this chapter at 2:27 a.m., feeling weary, if not faint, only to read that I will walk, yes, run, even soar, and have my strength renewed. At that hour? It hardly seemed possible. Yet He revived me then as He has so many times before.

Weariness is part of the human condition. Not my favorite part, but an undeniable one. Isaiah 40:30 reminds us, "Even youths grow tired and weary, and young men stumble and fall." God knows us well. Emotionally, physically, and spiritually, we all get tired; we all fall down.

Even the youngest among us. Even the strongest.

That woman in your Bible study who appears to have it all together? Perfect hair, great clothes, fresh manicure, with the questions in her workbook neatly answered? Trust me, she has bad-hair days, wrinkled-clothes days, broken-nail days, no-answers days. She may not let anybody see her that way, but, believe me, it happens.

Sometimes we try hard to look put together because inside we're falling apart. If you're there, here's good news right from the start of this verse.

But . . . *Isaiah 40:31*

One of my favorite words in the Bible, *but* signals change. It says, "The story isn't over yet." It encourages us to sit tight, to hang in there, knowing everything that's hard for us is easy for God.

. . . those who hope . . . *Isaiah 40:31*

Emily Dickinson wrote, "'Hope' is the thing with feathers / That perches in the soul."[1] Maybe she pictured a little black-capped chickadee, the state bird of her native Massachusetts. I need more hope than that. I need twelve pounds of bald eagle with seven thousand feathers. The kind of hope that has the power to lift us over the dry plains and barren deserts of our lives.

"Those who hope" is also translated as those "who expect, look for" (AMPC), whose eyes are drawn away from their troubles and in the direction of our God. Rest assured, "those who trust" (CEV) and "they that wait" (ASV) won't be disappointed.

Truth is, I can handle "No!" better than I can face "Wait." That's why our hope, our trust, our expectations belong here:

. . . in the LORD . . . *Isaiah 40:31*

Sometimes I put my hope in the wrong places. I look across the breakfast table at my dear husband or glance at my full speaking calendar or take in the view through our old farmhouse window. Blessings all, but not my source of hope.

People, position, possessions—none of them has the power to save us, and any of them could be gone from our lives tomorrow. The Lord alone offers us salvation. Like that huge bird full of hope, "He will cover you with his feathers, and under his wings you will find refuge"[2] and the power to go on.

. . . will renew their strength. *Isaiah 40:31*

We need emotional strength to weather whatever life throws at us, from toddlers to teenagers to tough employers. We need physical strength to tackle our long to-do lists and endless errands. Above all, we need spiritual strength to stand firm in our faith when others try to tear down what we know to be true.

If we "wait for the LORD's help" (NET), He assures us we'll "find new strength" (CEV) and a real source of "power" (AMP). Not within ourselves, but from Him. We literally "change strength" (WYC) from ours to His. Incredible.

With God in us and working through us, think of what we might accomplish for His kingdom!

They will soar on wings like eagles; . . . *Isaiah 40:31*

Too often we get our talons stuck in day-to-day worries when God is ready to lift us above all that. Can you sense the wind of His Spirit supporting you, transporting you? Life's troubles may not disappear from view, but at least we can get things in perspective when we see them from God's vantage point, high above the hassles.

And get this: female bald eagles are bigger than the males. Their bodies are about three feet long, and their wingspans can exceed seven feet. Seven feet, girlfriend! Imagine being that magnificent, that fierce, that strong as they "lift their wings" and "mount up to the sun" (AMPC).

Even staying closer to the ground and moving forward on two feet can work wonders.

> . . . they will run and not grow weary, . . . *Isaiah 40:31*

Every age has its own challenges and makes its own demands on our hearts, minds, and bodies. Let's resist the urge to say, "Oh, those old people!" or "Oh, those young people!" We help each other most not by comparing or criticizing but by pressing on together. If we "hasten, and never grow weary of hastening" (KNOX), we'll get where we want to go. Closer to one another. Closer to God.

> . . . they will walk and not be faint. *Isaiah 40:31*

With God's love and grace fueling our steps, He promises that we "won't get tired" (CJB) or "become weak" (NLV). When we feel weary, it's time to get our eyes off our problems and on God's Word. To listen to something uplifting and tell the Enemy of our souls to take a hike. To "march on, and never weaken on the march" (KNOX).

The sun's up now, and a new day has begun. Whatever the hours ahead may bring, God is ready to carry you through.

Heavenly Father,
when I'm overcome with weariness,
I will put my hope in You.
I'll imagine being lifted on Your wings,
carried high above my earthly cares
until they seem smaller, more manageable.
Then when my feet touch the ground,
I'll realize
You are the One who is
managing my life.

His Word, Your Heart

Tip #20 for memorizing Scripture:
Sing the verse to the tune of a familiar song.
Or create a simple rhythm you can tap out.

Isaiah 40:31 from the New International Version:

But those who hope in the LORD
will renew their strength.
They will soar on wings like eagles;
they will run and not grow weary,
they will walk and not be faint.

Isaiah 40:31 from your favorite translation:

21

Sharp Edge, Clean Cut

As iron sharpens iron,
so one person sharpens another.

PROVERBS 27:17

This verse is short, sweet, and . . . , um, sharp. Not only will we learn a bit about filing, whetting, and sanding, but we'll also discover why talking with a friend face to face can make all the difference.

As iron sharpens iron, . . . Proverbs 27:17

I've quoted this verse for years as if I knew what I was talking about. But the truth is, I'd never met a real blacksmith and had no idea how this sharpening business works. Now I do. In thirty seconds you will too.

The Word tells us "iron is made sharp with iron" (NLV), a process that begins with a standard metal file and an iron blade. The iron blade is propped on a support—say, a small wooden block—and then the metal file is drawn across the edge of the blade in slow, measured strokes until a sharp edge is created.

Next the "iron is whetted" (wyc) using a small amount of oil on a whetstone. Rubbing the iron blade against the oiled stone smoothes away the rough edge, leaving the blade polished and sharper still.

Then "in the same way that iron sharpens iron" (voice), heavy-duty sandpaper is cautiously smoothed along both sides of the blade. This blends the edge with the rest of the surface and makes the finished product exceedingly sharp.

Handle with care.

Sharp, pointy objects do a fine job of slicing bread for a meal or slicing the air in a sword fight. But they also can pierce our hearts and pry us open: "For the word of God is alive and active. Sharper than any double-edged sword, it penetrates even to dividing soul and spirit, joints and marrow; it judges the thoughts and attitudes of the heart."[1]

In our verse from Proverbs, the Hebrew word *barzel* means "iron tool." When we use our words like swords, we need to follow the Spirit's leading.

- Instead of cutting in two, open gently.
- Instead of rubbing the wrong way, polish.
- Instead of inflicting new wounds, smooth over the old ones.

. . . so one person sharpens another. *Proverbs 27:17*

The Hebrew word *rea* means not just any person but a "friend, companion, fellow, neighbor." Someone we know well. Someone we care about and who cares about us.

Our goal as believers is to hone one another so we become sharper and more effective in our faith. People opposed to God may "sharpen their tongues like swords,"[2] but those of us who love Him are called to "improve each other" (ncv).

Three centuries ago Matthew Henry said, "Wise and profitable discourse sharpens men's wits."[3] Still true today. Conversation—one on one, eye to eye—accomplishes far more than texting, tweeting, leaving messages, or sending e-mails.

After all, our faces talk too. Eyebrows rise with surprise or furrow with confusion. Mouths smile, frown, twist. Noses wrinkle. The Hebrew word *paneh* means "face." Literally, "friends sharpen each other's faces" (CEB). We smooth away the rough spots, not with sandpaper, but with wisdom. We "whetteth the face" (WYC) of a friend, not with a stone, but with a timely word.

The end result is better "character" (CJB) and sharper "minds" (CEV). Friends are meant to encourage one another and cheer on one another. Yet sometimes we have to say hard things and risk a friendship for the greater good.

After I had spoken at several Women of Faith conferences, two of my platform sisters approached me backstage and told me in no uncertain terms that I was no longer to make fun of my abundant body. "Own it, Liz. Don't trample it."

Oh my. What I thought was entertaining, even empowering, came off as self-deprecating and little else. *Ouch.* Still, these women knew me, loved me, and wanted God's best for me. However much the truth hurt, it was still the truth, and I took their wise counsel to heart.

It's so encouraging to know that "wounds from a friend can be trusted."[4] If your conscience has been pricked by someone who genuinely cares for you, keep this truth in mind: the words were meant to help and designed to heal. And if they were sent from God, they'll do both.

Another friend helped me see the error of my ways without saying a word. I'd exchanged presents with her through many holiday seasons, always hoping she enjoyed the gifts I'd chosen especially for her. She kindly returned the favor, sending me an equally thoughtful present, until one Christmas when all I received was a card with a note: "I gave a donation to this wonderful charity in your name."

My first response? *Humph. This isn't a gift. It's a tax write-off.* (Sorry. That's the sad truth of it.) I kept looking at the donor card, trying to get excited about the idea and failing miserably.

Finally the Lord opened my eyes.

Do you need yet another present, Liz? I do not.

Do impoverished families need help? They do.

Whether she did so by intent or by accident, my friend had provided the gift I needed most: fresh eyes to see my shortsightedness and a chance to follow her good example. If someone has given you a new way of looking at things, maybe it's time to return the favor. And pass it on.

Father God,
thank You for all my sword-bearing friends.
They open Your Word to me when I need it most,
and they close my mouth when I need that.
Help me be as brave and loving as my friends are.
Help me not only speak Your truth in love
but also live out Your truth in deed.

His Word, Your Heart

Tip #21 for memorizing Scripture:
Make it personal.
Mine your memory for a life experience
that illustrates the verse.

Proverbs 27:17 from the New International Version:

As iron sharpens iron,
so one person sharpens another.

Proverbs 27:17 from your favorite translation:

22

Perfect Peace

*You will keep in perfect peace
those whose minds are steadfast,
because they trust in you.*

ISAIAH 26:3

ay 2013 was a hard month in Oklahoma. Tornadoes claimed too many loved ones, demolished too many homes, tore apart too many lives. When I opened the Bible in search of a word of comfort to post on social media, I read the above verse from Isaiah with a lump firmly lodged in my throat.

Yes, Lord. Your peace is perfect. Then I realized these words are actually lyrics to an ancient song. This chapter in Scripture begins "In that day this song will be sung in the land of Judah."[1] What day was Isaiah talking about? The day of judgment on the earth.

A terrible day for those who turned their backs on God.

A glorious day for those who put their trust in Him.

Beloved, that day is going to come more surely, swiftly, and catastrophically than any tornado. Even so, God assures His people that we will find peace in the eye of the storm.

There are just sixteen words in this verse, but every one is packed with hope. I'll try not to wear you out with this, but, seriously, every word matters. Look.

You . . . *Isaiah 26:3*

This is "the LORD" (CEV). He is the only One who can make and keep the promise that's about to unfold. If we look for lasting peace elsewhere, we won't find it. If we think any government in the world can provide it, we are fooling ourselves.

Only God. Only, only God.

. . . will . . . *Isaiah 26:3*

Not *maybe*. Not *probably*. Not *shoulda, coulda, woulda*. He *will*.

In fact, He "dost" (RSV). It's a promise that has already been fulfilled in Him and by Him. "I know that everything God does will endure forever."[2] *Forever* means eternity in both directions. All the way back and all the way forward. Beyond the parameters of time as we know it.

This is the pledge Eternal God has made to His people: *I will*.

Unfortunately I make—and break—a dozen promises a day. "I'll be right there." "I'm almost done." "I'll get back to you soon." I mean well, but I don't always deliver. *Soon* becomes two hours later, two days later, two weeks later. *Almost done* is worthless until you reach *done*.

When God says He will, He will.

. . . keep . . . *Isaiah 26:3*

How I love being a kept woman when God is the One doing the keeping! He will "give" (NIrV) and "guard" (AMPC); He will "preserve" (CJB) and "protect" (LEB).

The safest place for me to store my wedding ring is on my hand, where it won't be lost or stolen. This is what God does to keep us close: "See, I have engraved you on the palms of my hands."[3] Right here. Touch. See.

. . . in perfect . . . *Isaiah 26:3*

Perfect doesn't mean we get it right. It means God gets it right. "As for God, his way is perfect."[4] And His perfection leads to a destination we all long for.

. . . peace . . . *Isaiah 26:3*

Some translations point out how perfect His peace is by doubling it: "peace, peace" (EXB), "shalom shalom" (OJB). Like squaring a number, it's peace to the second power. "Peace, peace, to those far and near."[5] Peace is what everyone wants and few experience. "The peace of God, which transcends all understanding."[6] Exactly so.

What gives us a deep sense of peace? Knowing we are in the center of God's will. How can we be sure we're there? "The God of our ancestors has chosen you to know his will."[7] The more peaceful we are, and the longer we wait before Him in the stillness of prayer, the clearer His will becomes. Since "the LORD decides where we will go,"[8] we can trust Him to show us the way.

. . . those . . . *Isaiah 26:3*

It's not very personal sounding, but *those* means *us:* His followers, His believers, His children, His own. Those who know God's peace. Those who have taken the next step, not with their feet, but with their heads.

. . . whose minds . . . *Isaiah 26:3*

My mind can get me into serious trouble. Though my heart belongs completely to God, my mind sometimes meanders off course. Seeking credit. Needing attention. Hoping to impress. Wanting to wow. Left unchecked by the Spirit, my mind drifts into dark alleys where jealousy and envy lurk and self-pity sticks out its big foot to trip me up.

God's sure solution? "Set your minds on things above, not on earthly things."[9] When His life-giving Word is our focus, then our thoughts have a safe place to land.

. . . are steadfast, . . . *Isaiah 26:3*

I love how the word *are* sweeps away any sense of *maybe*. And *steadfast*? I could go a whole year and never use that word outside of a Bible study. We might say *steady* or *faithful,* but *steadfast* bears more weight. A steadfast mind that's "stayed on thee" (ASV) produces "sound thoughts" (CEB) and helps people "maintain their faith" (NET). That's how He keeps our minds from wobbling out of control.

. . . because . . . *Isaiah 26:3*

We're about to learn the why, the answer, the *because.* It's the whole of the Christian life on the head of a nail driven into the flesh of the One who lived and died and rose again so we would believe and love and have faith.

. . . they trust . . . *Isaiah 26:3*

The *T* word. It's woven all through Scripture and all through these pages as well. *Trust* means putting down my shield of defense and letting God fight my battles: the battles in my mind, the battles in my flesh, and the battles in my heart. For those of us who have trust issues, this verse is our way out. Better yet, our way *in.*

. . . in . . . *Isaiah 26:3*

Yes, even the tiny word *in* matters. It's impossible to simply trust. You have to trust *in* something or Someone. "In you they trusted and were not put to shame."[10]

Everything we've been learning points here.

. . . you. *Isaiah 26:3*

The last word of this verse is the same as the first. *You,* Lord. You are the only One who can give us perfect peace in the midst of our storms.

Heavenly Father,
You have certainly proven trustworthy.
From the day I embraced Your gift of grace,
You have shown me the beauty of Your peace.
Help me dial down the drama.
Help me rest and not resist.
Help me trust You in all things.

His Word, Your Heart

Isaiah 26:3 from the New International Version:

You will keep in perfect peace
those whose minds are steadfast,
because they trust in you.

Isaiah 26:3 from your favorite translation:

23

Start to Finish

Being confident of this,
that he who began a good work in you
will carry it on to completion
until the day of Christ Jesus.

PHILIPPIANS 1:6

*I*f you are independent, are always in a hurry, and like to be in charge, this verse might push a few buttons. (My hand is up.) If you are a team player, are happy to wait your turn, and don't care who gets credit, you're going to love every word.

Our verse starts in the middle of a sentence, so we need to back up a few lines to catch the wave of emotion flowing here. "I thank my God every time I remember you. In all my prayers for all of you, I always pray with joy because of your partnership in the gospel from the first day until now."[1]

Such wonderful sentiments. Gratitude. Remembrance. Joy. Paul was writing to the saints in Philippi, assuring them that he gave thanks to the Lord whenever they crossed his mind. No criticizing their weaknesses or failures, no requests for God to fix them, no complaints about their stewardship. Paul insisted that praying for them made him "happy."[2]

I'm thinking of a pastor I met years ago who invited my husband and me to join him in his office before the service. We thought we were gathering to pray. Instead, the pastor spent fifteen minutes grumbling about his congregation and running them down by name. No wonder his flock was dwindling each week! My heart ached for them and also for him. Bitterness is a hard weed to yank out once it takes root.

In good soil, though, joy flourishes. Our own pastor recently wrote us to say, "Of all the things I do in my role as pastor, the most important and humbling task is my call to pray for God's people."

Okay, *that* is what Paul was talking about: spending time in prayer with a full awareness of its value. He was especially excited about the Philippians' mutual "furtherance of the gospel"[3] and the ways they "shared in proclaiming the Good News."[4] Paul's enthusiasm then can become our passion now: To minister as a circle of friends, as a discipleship group, as a mission team, as a church. To sense God's Spirit moving among us, working through us, accomplishing His will. To know we're partnering with like-minded people for a cause far greater than ourselves. Thrilling beyond description!

From "day one"[5] when Paul showed up talking about Jesus, the believers in Philippi embraced the truth and shared his vision. They told everyone who would listen, they participated in a hands-on way, and they ushered friends and neighbors into God's kingdom.

Because of all the above—all the prayers, all the joy, all the fellowship—Paul was certain of their success.

Being confident of this, . . . *Philippians 1:6*

Paul was "convinced" (AMP); he was "persuaded" (EXB); he was "sure about this" (CEB). "There has never been the slightest doubt in my mind" (MSG), he told them. He'd planted healthy seeds and watched them sprout.

He saw proof of their growth. His confidence was based on evidence rather than just a feel-good emotion.

We can scarcely measure our own spiritual growth. We know our flaws too well and realize how far we still have to go. If someone has watched our walk with the Lord—a pastor, a teacher, a parent—and says, "You've really grown spiritually," we may find that hard to believe.

Believe, my friend.

. . . *that he who began a good work in you . . . Philippians 1:6*

Clearly, "God is the one who began this good work" (CEV): This desire to partner with other believers. This eagerness to share the gospel. This willingness to share resources. The good work God began in us might include making us less self-sufficient and more dependent on Him. Less rushed and more relaxed. Less likely to take charge, more likely to follow and support.

The me-me-me, go-go-go approach to life is of no use to God. Pliable, flexible, adaptable—that's what He's looking for. For all of us who aren't there yet, God is patiently shaping, molding, waiting.

. . . *will carry it on to completion . . . Philippians 1:6*

God's work in us "will continue" (AMPC), and He won't quit until it reaches "perfection" (KNOX). What a relief! I've never finished any project and thought it was truly complete. I'd love to rewrite every book I've written and redo every speech I've given. But that's not how it works. We simply release our work to God and trust Him with the outcome.

Even so, God will "go on developing" (Phillips) His children. He will "stay with you to complete the job" (CEB). He won't "stop in mid-design but will keep perfecting you" (VOICE).

The best parent on his or her best day cannot come close to what our heavenly Father does for us all day, every day.

When a toddler is mastering a new skill—say, eating with a spoon—the whole messy process could be avoided if Mom just continued spooning in each mouthful. But that's not the loving thing to do. The loving thing is to give a child the right tools, then eat with her, side by side. Show her by example. Patiently correct the way she holds the spoon. Let her try again and again. Make certain she doesn't spoon in too much at once. Retrieve the spoon after she flings it across the kitchen.

God is waiting and willing to teach even those of us who are prone to flinging spoons out of sheer frustration. He never gives up. He never lets go. He never stops delighting in His children.

It's just as well we can't measure His truth taking root in us—the strength of our branches, the sweetness of our fruit—because it's God's work, not our work. His doing, not our doing. Only God "will keep it growing" (cjb) until it's time for the harvest.

> . . . until the day of Christ Jesus. *Philippians 1:6*

Does this mean a specific day? Yes, it does. The very day, the very hour when "Christ Jesus returns" (cev), "the final day of judgment and reward" (exb), "the day when Jesus Christ comes again" (erv).

My friend Gail is involved in a Bible study with a new believer who was stunned to learn that the Lord will return someday. Perched on the edge of her seat, eyes as big as saucers, she exclaimed, "Jesus is coming *back*?" Indeed He is, sister!

Until that day we're not working with the final package. God will continue His efforts "right up to the time of His return" (ampc). He is still pruning, shaping, and fertilizing our faith. That last splash of water, that last snip of His shears will come at the moment of His Son's return. He will "bring it to a flourishing finish on the very day Christ Jesus appears" (msg).

No wonder Philippians 1:6 is a favorite of so many believers. It's all

God, it's all good, and it's all done when He says it is. Meanwhile, He is for you, with you, and at work in you.

And all the people of God whispered, *"Whew."*

Lord God,
when I think of all
You are accomplishing
through those who love You,
I am glad to play a tiny part
in Your great big adventure.
And I'm truly grateful
You continue to work in me.
I need You every hour, Lord.

His Word, Your Heart

Tip #23 for memorizing Scripture:
Add the verse below your signature
on e-mails and letters.

Philippians 1:6 from the New International Version:

Being confident of this,
that he who began a good work in you
will carry it on to completion
until the day of Christ Jesus.

Philippians 1:6 from your favorite translation:

24

With You

Have I not commanded you?
Be strong and courageous.
Do not be afraid; do not be discouraged,
for the LORD your God will be
with you wherever you go.

JOSHUA 1:9

When I feel weak, uncertain, vulnerable, the last thing I want is someone telling me, "Be strong!" That's like saying to spaghetti, "Stand up!" Even fresh out of the box, those dry, slender strands can't perch on end.

Go ahead. Shout out all the affirming words you like. "Get up!" "You can do it!" "I believe in you!" Not happening. Pasta down. But let a master chef step into the picture, and everything changes. The spaghetti is easily held upright, secure in his grip.

That's the essence of this verse. Not that you can be strong and brave if you try. Rather, you are strong and brave for one reason: the Lord goes with you.

Joshua 1:9 is another remarkable quote from God, who spoke these words to Joshua, Moses's right-hand man. After Moses died, God told Joshua to lead His people across the Jordan River into Israel. The words God used to empower His servant Joshua are meant to strengthen our hearts today.

We're listening, Lord.

Have I not commanded you? *Joshua 1:9*

No doubt who's in charge, right? Joshua may be leading the people, but God is leading Joshua. "Haven't I ordered you" (cjb), the Lord asks. "Did I not command you?" (leb).

If our strength comes from His strength—and it does—then this reminder of His authority is the right place to begin. Yes, God is our Comforter, but He is also our Commander in Chief. He has every right to say, "That is what I ask of thee" (knox).

God had made this request of Joshua twice before, in verses 6 and 7, which is why this phrase is sometimes translated "remember" (erv) or "I repeat" (net). So what is this message God wants to make sure Joshua hears—and we hear—loud and clear?

Be strong and courageous. *Joshua 1:9*

Two powerful words: "Strength! Courage!" (msg). We could look at them separately, but they're meant to go together like salt and pepper. God calls us to be "determined and confident!" (gnt), to be "strong and brave!" (net), to "have strength of heart!" (nlv). Lots of exclamation points here. God is serious about this.

He is also the One who does the heavy lifting. He provides the muscle, the tendons, the sinew. The power and strength are His alone. He commands us to be, as the Hebrew word *amets* captures it, "stout, strong, bold, alert" because He is all these things and more.

However strong a bodybuilder may be, eventually he or she will have to lower those heavy weights to the floor. But God never lets go. God never gives up.

Do not be afraid; . . . *Joshua 1:9*

God's people didn't know what they would find on the other side of the Jordan River. Naturally, they were afraid. But, supernaturally, they didn't need to be. God was already in Israel, waiting to welcome them home even as He walked beside them as they traveled there.

What was true for His people thousands of years ago is true for us now. God not only knows our future. He not only holds our future. He *is* our future. That's why He tells us, "Don't be alarmed" (CEB) and "Don't be timid" (MSG). That's why He asks us not to "tremble" (NASB) or "be terrified" (AMP).

When I first began speaking publicly, I was a nervous wreck. Icy hands, dry mouth, shaky knees—the whole bit. After five hundred speeches I realized I wasn't quite so scared anymore. God truly was with me, just as He is with you, all the time.

Letting go of fear is a process. It doesn't happen overnight. But it does happen. In the meantime God urges us to keep the faith.

. . . do not be discouraged, . . . *Joshua 1:9*

"I've already tried that."

"Nothing seems to work."

"What difference does it make?"

We know those words. We've said them, thought them, repeated them. But God says, "Do not lose hope" (NIrv). He doesn't want us to be "dismayed" (DRA) or "downhearted" (CJB).

Because of His great compassion, He gives us the ultimate confidence booster.

. . . for . . . *Joshua 1:9*

This small word is the turning point in the verse. "Because" (NCV) gives things more heft. "When" (KNOX) gives us greater assurance.

Strength and courage are possible *because* . . .

Fear and discouragement are no longer a stumbling block *when* . . .

. . . the LORD your God . . . *Joshua 1:9*

Not just any god, but your God. The One we call "Jehovah" (ASV), the One we know as "*ADONAI*" (CJB).

. . . will be with you . . . *Joshua 1:9*

It's a promise of God, meaning it's a finished work. He "is with thee" (ASV), He "is at thy side" (KNOX), and He "will remain with you" (VOICE). Look before, behind, and around you, and God is there.

This means God is with you at this very moment. Whether you are sitting or standing, working or resting, having breakfast or dinner, spending time alone or with company, He is there.

. . . wherever you go. *Joshua 1:9*

He's not only where you are now, but He will travel with you "every step you take" (MSG), "anywhere you go" (NLV), and "in all you do" (NET).

The Hebrew word *halak* used here in Joshua also poured from Ruth's mouth when she made her remarkable pledge to Naomi: "whither thou goest, I will go."[1] Literally it means "in all manner" you "go, come, walk."

The bad news? You can't go anywhere without God. Those of us who've tried to run from Him know how pointless it is. His love is too strong, His patience unfathomable.

The good news? God won't go anywhere without you. You are His, and He is yours. Forever.

Lord God,
sometimes I forget that You are with me.
I allow fears to overwhelm me
and discouragement to undermine me.
Open my eyes.
Help me see You
in Your Word,
in Your people,
in Your creation.
Prompt me to read this verse
over and over
until the truth sinks in:
You always go with me.

His Word, Your Heart

Joshua 1:9 from the New International Version:

Have I not commanded you?
Be strong and courageous.
Do not be afraid; do not be discouraged,
for the LORD your God will be
with you wherever you go.

Joshua 1:9 from your favorite translation:

25

Flawless

Every word of God is flawless;
he is a shield to those who take refuge in him.

PROVERBS 30:5

Being airbrushed for a video shoot was a weird sensation. I sat absolutely still while a fine mist of ivory liquid swept across my skin. "Ah," the makeup pro said at last, smiling at her work. "Flawless."

Nice try, sister. All the cosmetics in the world can't hide our many imperfections—inside or out. When it comes to being flawless, there's only one place to look.

Every word of God . . . Proverbs 30:5

I love how the Bible makes this crystal clear. Not some words, not most words, but "all God's words" (CEB) are counted here. "Everything God says" (CEV) and "every word that God speaks" (ERV) is perfect, finished, complete. The proof? "God keeps every promise he makes" (GNT).

I don't know a soul who has kept every promise he or she made. Not my parents, not my teachers, not my siblings, not my friends, not even my darling husband. And I hate to think of how many times I've neglected to follow through on my promises.

We all drop the ball now and again. But God? Never.

. . . is flawless; . . . *Proverbs 30:5*

Even beautiful diamonds have flaws, but God's Word is "pure" (CJB) and "perfect" (NIrV). We know this, not only because He says so, but also because His Word has been "tested" (NASB) and "fire tried" (DRA). Not in a blacksmith's forge but in real life.

When fear starts to creep into my heart or skitter up my spine, I turn to His Word and read it aloud: "For I am the LORD your God who takes hold of your right hand and says to you, Do not fear; I will help you."[1] Then I take His promise and run with it. I tell that stubborn fear, "God is here." I stand still, breathing quietly and listening intently, until I sense God's presence, just as the Bible describes.

When we take God at His word and trust what He has promised, He "proves true" (ESV) and "passes the test" (EXB) every time. Have you tried Him? Then you know God always has your back. "He will never leave you nor forsake you."[2]

God might make you wait, but He never makes you wait alone. How can we be sure? Jesus said, "I am not alone, for my Father is with me."[3] God is our Father as well, and He offers the same assurance to His children. "You have not abandoned any who seek you, LORD."[4]

I think I just heard a huge sigh of relief. And it gets better.

. . . he is a shield . . . *Proverbs 30:5*

In Hebrew, *magen* means a literal shield, which is why the six-pointed Star of David is more properly known as the Shield of David or Magen David. Who carries shields? Soldiers. Protectors. Knights. Defenders.

And God, who "guards" (NCV) us with "a shield set afire" (WYC). What enemy would dare come near a mighty God with a flaming shield!

. . . to those who take refuge in him. *Proverbs 30:5*

His refuge offers a "safe place" (ERV) for us. We just have to be willing to run to the Lord and let Him handle things.

This is where I get into trouble. Miss Do-It-All-by-Myself says, "I've got this. No problem. Here, hold my latte." Then I tackle, say, a difficult e-mail (the kind that starts out "I don't mean to criticize you, but . . ."), and I forget to consult God before answering. My first draft sounds defensive, and the second sounds petulant until I finally turn to God for help. Only then do my words sound more like His words—compassionate and understanding—instead of grumpy and childish.

Still, think of all the wasted time and unnecessary teeth grinding we could avoid if we simply ducked behind His shield in the first place, if we said, "I trust You for the perfect words, Lord. Please tell me what to say."

Who's welcome to step behind His shield? The people who "hope in him" (DRA) and "put their trust in him" (KJV), the ones who "come to him for safety" (CEV) and "seek his protection" (GNT). It's a big shield, my friend. God, the creator of heaven and earth, is the One holding it, providing "a safe-covering" (NLV) for all who are willing to admit they need His help.

Some of us have been bruised by abuse. Broken by disappointment. Weighed down by depression. We don't think we're worth protecting, worth rescuing. But the Lord says of every one of His people, "You are precious and honored in my sight."[5]

Have you been redeemed by His righteousness? Made whole by His holiness? Set free by His sacrifice? Then you can jump behind His shield anytime. In fact, you can live there, safe and secure, the whole of your life.

Does that mean you're weak? Not at all. It means you're made strong in Him.

Heavenly Father,
how comforting to realize I am
never alone, never defenseless.
You hide me behind Your shield.
You hold my fears at bay.
You fill me with
Your flawless Word.
You never abandon me.
You keep me safe.

His Word, Your Heart

> **Tip #25 for memorizing Scripture:**
> Put the verse where you'll see it daily—
> the more locations, the better.

Proverbs 30:5 from the New International Version:
Every word of God is flawless;
he is a shield to those who take refuge in him.

Proverbs 30:5 from your favorite translation:

26

Love Mercy

He has shown you, O mortal, what is good.
And what does the LORD require of you?
To <u>act justly</u> and to <u>love mercy</u>
and to <u>walk humbly</u> with your God.

MICAH 6:8

Some of us like to keep things simple. Just tell us what to do, and we'll do it. Especially when we've messed up, we want a list showing us how to fix what's broken. One, two, three. Check off each one and we're done.

God tucks a short to-do list like that among the pages of Micah, a small book full of big themes. Big, bad themes, actually. The coming judgment. Weeping and mourning. False prophets and dishonest leaders. Guilt and punishment. Misery and desolation. Hard to believe this much-loved verse falls in the middle of all that.

Is there any good news? Any hope of redemption? Oh yes. In the meantime, to quote Bette Davis in the classic movie *All About Eve*, "Fasten your seat belts. It's going to be a bumpy night."

In the eighth century BC, "The word of the LORD ... came to Micah,"[1] a minor prophet from the hill country south of Jerusalem. The role of a prophet is to speak God's truth even when people find it painful to hear. During Micah's day idolatry was rampant, spiritual lethargy was pandemic, and justice and fairness were nowhere to be found.

Sound familiar?

At the start of Micah 6, God takes the bench, gavel in hand: "For the LORD has a case against his people; he is lodging a charge against Israel."[2] After the charges are outlined, the chapter ends with a stiff sentence: "Therefore I will give you over to ruin and your people to derision."[3] Though it sounds harsh, God's people were without excuse. He had made His expectations clear.

He has shown you, O mortal, . . . *Micah 6:8*

There's a phrase we don't toss around very much: "O mortal." In the Bible it's seldom used as a compliment since "God is greater than any mortal."[4] The book of Job gives mortals a sound thrashing, describing us as "full of trouble,"[5] "vile and corrupt,"[6] "a maggot . . . a worm!"[7] *Ewww.*

Unlike immortal God, mortals are "men and women" (MSG), who will die. God declares, "Return to dust, you mortals."[8] Our mortality, our fragility, our finality—all are abundantly clear.

God is not so gently reminding us here that "the life of mortals is like grass . . . the wind blows over it and it is gone, and its place remembers it no more."[9] Ever walked through a cemetery filled with old gravestones? Could you read the names once carved in granite? In the same way, the departed are "no more." However valiantly they served God's purposes on earth, those who've gone before us are . . . well, gone.

Then the darkness begins to lift.

. . . what is good. *Micah 6:8*

God is showing us "what is good in His sight" (VOICE). Not good by our definition, but good by His definition. My standard of what's good is all over the map. I compare one behavior with another instead of comparing everything I do with God's goodness, and I end up with actions that are pretty good, not so good, kinda good—

No, Liz. *Good* is what God says is good: Himself.

In fact, Jesus said, "No one is good—except God alone."[10] Why do we insist on making up our own rules when God has already laid down the law?

And what does the LORD require of you? *Micah 6:8*

We often prefer to go with the bare minimum. That's what the Israelites were doing during Micah's time: asking for the cut-to-the-chase list of "what *ADONAI* demands" (CJB) and "what the LORD really wants" (NET). We're right there with them. We want to know "how to live, what to do, what GOD is looking for" (MSG)—as long as His requirements are manageable. As long as we don't actually have to change.

Lord, help us. Please.

To act justly . . . *Micah 6:8*

That's the first of three items on God's list. "See that justice is done" (CEV), He tells us. "Be fair to other people" (ERV). "Do what is right" (NLT). Sounds easy enough. Be fair; play nice; do random acts of kindness. Is that it?

No. We need to think bigger. Think broader. Think how to "promote justice" (NET) in every corner of the world we touch. Some people I know excel at this. They volunteer. They give away their time and talents and resources. They reach out to the least of these and find themselves touching the hem of Christ's garment.

When we focus on everybody getting a fair share instead of making sure we keep what's ours, we show the world a God who loves the poor and lifts up the humble and embraces the broken. We show them Jesus.

We can't do everything for everyone. But we can do something for ✈ someone.

. . . and to love mercy . . . *Micah 6:8*

This one seems easier to follow. "Love grace" (CJB)? You bet. "Love being kind to others" (EXB)? With all my heart, Lord. "Let mercy be your first concern" (CEV)? I'm in. Let's go.

Sadly, my desire to extend mercy, grace, kindness, and compassion to others eventually runs out. Like a switch being flicked off, I'm suddenly out of juice, out of energy, out of spare minutes. Though the Word commands us to "love one another" about a dozen times, I find myself saying, "Can I pass on this one today, Lord? Can You find another person to love her? Someone who isn't weary of doing good right now?"

He patiently reminds me of what I already know: with God I can do anything. So I've learned how to stay plugged in. A quick nap for my tired body helps. A quiet time of prayer refreshes my soul. Then after a cool drink of living water from the Word, I'm ready to dive back in.

Live
. . . and to walk humbly . . . *Micah 6:8*

A handful of words yet a huge challenge. "Walk" is the translation we find most, yet "live" (NCV) and "obey" (ERV) help us move beyond the physical act of walking to grasp what God is really saying.

Step by step He enables us to live a life that's holy, set apart. To follow His lead and love others. To put feet to our faith and do it humbly, like a child who knows he is a child and so depends on his parents. "These are the ones I look on with favor: those who are humble and contrite in spirit, and who tremble at my word."[11]

This is what He wants: a people who tremble with awe when His

Word is spoken, who see His power at work in their corner of the world and are humbled.

> . . . with your God. *Micah 6:8*

Your God, the "True God" (voice), the "one God and Father of all, who is over all and through all and in all."[12] We may fail, but God never fails. He is with us, and we're with Him.

After the prophet Micah thoroughly chastised God's people, he ended his final chapter by praising the Lord for His grace, saying, "You will again have compassion on us; you will tread our sins underfoot and hurl all our iniquities into the depths of the sea."[13]

Read that verse aloud and let the truth of it sink in. *Into the depths of the sea.* That's where God has tossed all your failures, all your mistakes, all your sins. All of them. No need to go deep-sea diving, trying to retrieve your past and drag it back to shore. God has taken care of it. Every trace is gone. For good.

Father God,
thank You for showing me what is good.
Even more,
thank You for being
goodness itself.
What You ask of me is clear, Lord.
When my flesh is weak,
strengthen me.
When my love runs out,
love through me.
When I'm full of myself,
empty me.

His Word, Your Heart

Tip #26 for memorizing Scripture:
Carry the verse in your purse
for easy review.

Micah 6:8 from the New International Version:

He has shown you, O mortal, what is good.
And what does the LORD require of you?
To act justly and to love mercy
and to walk humbly with your God.

Micah 6:8 from your favorite translation:

ESV
He has told you, O man, what is
good.
and what does the Lord require of
you?
but to <u>do</u> justice, and to love kindness,
and to walk humbly with your God

27

Fearless

But now, this is what the LORD says—
he who created you, Jacob,
he who formed you, Israel:
"Do not fear, for I have redeemed you;
I have summoned you by name; you are mine."

ISAIAH 43:1

Fear can stalk us, linger in the shadows, track us down, paralyze us. Sometimes our fears are nameless, faceless. And sometimes we know exactly why we're afraid and who or what we dread most.

Yet God says throughout His Word, "Do not fear." Can we really live unafraid?

The verse above acknowledges that fears exist, then shows us the permanent solution God offers. Get a steak knife, sister, because this is some serious meat.

But now, . . . *Isaiah 43:1*

If only we didn't have these two simple words, we could dive right in and not look back. We could start with the good news, the happy ending, and not worry about what came before—the bad news, the unhappy beginning. "And now" (DRA) or "Now this" (EXB) softens the blow, but either way we can tell something important came right before our chosen verse.

The end of the previous chapter in Isaiah is all about being spiritually lost, utterly deaf, and stubbornly blind to the things of God. The words are strong, uncompromising. The kind that make you wince. "You have seen many things, but you pay no attention; your ears are open, but you do not listen."[1]

We don't usually choose such verses as our go-to favorites. They convict us, as they're meant to. They make us see ourselves as we really are. And because of that, they are a generous gift from the Holy Spirit. (Yes, really.) We need to know we're lost before we can celebrate being found. We need to understand we're deaf before we can truly hear. And we need to realize we're blind before we can rejoice at being able to see.

So the Lord made it plain to His people: "Hear, you deaf; look, you blind, and see!"[2] Why would a loving God speak so bluntly? Because His genuine love for people means He will do whatever it takes to help us grow. We can't grow if we don't let Him examine our unhealthy roots and fertilize them with His truth. And we can't bloom where God has planted us if we don't allow the Gardener to prune our dead branches.

One translation sums up the phrase "But now" like this: "in spite of past judgments for Israel's sins" (AMPC). Are you thinking, *Hey, I'm not Israel*? If you belong to God, then you've been grafted in with His people.[3] Though this message from the prophet Isaiah was aimed at God's followers who would be exiled in Babylon, the truths found here are for all God's people in all generations, including ours.

. . . this is what the LORD says— . . . *Isaiah 43:1*

Anytime we spot this phrase in Scripture, our hearts are meant to stir with anticipation. "Here is a message" (KNOX), we're told, so let's "listen to the LORD" (NLT) and hear what He has for us.

> . . . he who created you, Jacob, he who formed you,
> Israel: . . . *Isaiah 43:1*

Oh, Jacob. What a troublemaker! A fraternal twin, he entered the world "grasping Esau's heel,"[4] demanding to have his own way from birth. No wonder *Jacob* has come to mean "supplanter," "schemer," "wrestler," "finagler," "deceiver."

Even so, God loved Jacob. Stayed by his side. Told him, "I am with you and will watch over you wherever you go"[5] right after Jacob stole his brother's inheritance. Then after God wrestled with Jacob, He changed Jacob's name as further proof of His mercy: "Your name will no longer be Jacob, but Israel."[6]

"Deceiver" became "triumphant with God." Wow.

That's the God we're talking about here, the One who created Jacob the person, then fashioned Israel the people. Whenever we see "the God of Jacob," it's a reminder of what a grace-giving Lord we serve.

Now the good news you've been waiting for.

> . . . "Do not fear, . . ." *Isaiah 43:1*

- If we fear a life of insignificance, God says, "Fear not" (ASV).
- If we fear losing our relationship with Him, God says, "Don't be afraid" (CJB).
- If we dread illness, sorrow, or death, God says, "Do not thou dread" (WYC).
- If we fear loneliness, God says, "You have nothing to fear" (VOICE).

- If we fear punishment for our sins, God says, "Be not afraid" (YLT).
- If we're afraid of not making it to heaven, God says, "You must not fear" (LEB).

". . . for I have redeemed you; . . ." *Isaiah 43:1*

Because of His mercy and grace, our salvation and redemption are a finished work. And look how personal God's promise is! "I have rescued you" (CEV). "I have ransomed you" (NLT). "I have bought you and made you free" (NLV).

What have we done? We've been deaf, blind, lost.

What has God done? Paid the price. Redeemed us. Bought us back. "I again-bought thee" (WYC). Like purchasing something, only to have it stolen from your home, then tracking it down it at a yard sale and willingly buying it a second time.

That's how precious you are to God. He redeemed His own creation.

". . . I have summoned you by name; . . ." *Isaiah 43:1*

Still on a personal note, God says, "I have called you by your name" (AMPC). And what is that name? His.

". . . you are mine." *Isaiah 43:1*

Your name is I Belong to Almighty God. Your name is I Am the Lord's Servant.

"You are Mine!" (NLV) God says. And "you belong to me" (CEV). One translation simply says "thou Mine" (YLT). It's the ultimate promise from God. More sacred than a marriage vow, more lasting than any family name.

The next time you're feeling unnoticed, unimportant, unloved, unclaimed, let this truth resonate in your heart and mind, dear sister. The Creator sees you, values you, loves you, and calls you His.

Heavenly Father,
on days when I seem to have
lost my way,
when I feel
blind to Your truth
and deaf to Your voice,
please summon me afresh.
Speak my name.
Call me Yours.

His Word, Your Heart

> **Tip #27 for memorizing Scripture:**
> Write the verse on a flashcard,
> put the reference on the flip side,
> and then have others test you.

Isaiah 43:1 from the New International Version:

But now, this is what the LORD says—
he who created you, Jacob,
he who formed you, Israel:
"Do not fear, for I have redeemed you;
I have summoned you by name; you are mine."

Isaiah 43:1 from your favorite translation:

vs redeem!

Good News: Isreil, The Lord who
created you says "Do not be
afraid — I will save you. I have
Called you by name — you are mine.

28

Right Answer

A person finds joy in giving an apt reply—
and how good is a timely word!

PROVERBS 15:23

Remember how great it felt to raise your hand in school when you knew the right answer? You couldn't wait for the teacher to call on you, couldn't wait to hear "Well done!"

Is it much different now when you're in a Bible study and the leader asks someone to share what she has learned from a passage? *Pick me, pick me.*

When God gives us the right words to say, we need to speak up. But if we're not careful, we'll be *that girl*—showing off, seeking to impress, forgetting where her knowledge or insight came from in the first place. Those of us who love to hear the sound of our own voices (we know who we are) especially need to choose our words with care.

A person finds joy . . . *Proverbs 15:23*

Joy is an all-good thing. No calories, no cost, no worries, no downside. Good for the body, good for the soul. The Hebrew word *simchah* means "gladness, mirth," so we're talking a serious party. Not just short-lived happiness, but "great joy" (voice) that lasts forever. It's also universal, something "everyone enjoys" (nlt).

But there's a catch. Our joy is meant to be outward focused as we do everything for the good of someone else rather than for ourselves. The "pleasure" (msg) we experience is a by-product of doing the right thing. Or, in this case, *saying* the right thing.

Want more joy in your life? Speak words that bless others.

> . . . in giving an apt reply— . . .
> *Proverbs 15:23*

If "apt reply" sounds a bit stuffy, "a good answer" (erv) or "good advice" (exb) helps us grasp the point of the proverb, which I believe is this: when people ask you a question and the answer you give them is "appropriate" (ceb) or "fitting" (nlt) or "suitable" (wyc), the Lord has used you to dish out a blessing.

So who gets the glory for this apt reply? God alone. Our job is to point the applause in His direction.

As a writer I find that my words come slowly, with much gnashing of teeth. Those are not the words people usually remember. But when the Holy Spirit steps forward and breathes life into a writer's work, words come more quickly and bear more fruit. Readers have shown me which sentences in my books they've underlined, and with few exceptions they are the phrases God kindly whispered in my ear.

Maybe you've had a similar experience:

- A friend asks you a tough spiritual question. Almost
  effortlessly a wise and biblical answer pours out of
  your mouth, one that meets her needs and addresses

her problem. Stunned, you think, *Where did that come from?* But you already know the answer.

- You're invited to teach a class at church, so you carefully prepare your lesson. Then right in the middle of teaching, you offer some new insight that's not in your notes. The class nods, makes affirming noises, maybe even claps. All the while you're thinking, *Wow, I need to write that down.* Yes, you do.

- The family member you've been praying for, the one who has been running from God, suddenly reaches out to you, desperate for His forgiveness. With a clear head and a surprisingly calm heart, you share the good news and then watch in wonder as God welcomes your loved one into His kingdom.

When such things happen, you feel as if you're standing on holy ground, yes? "Joy belongs to a man with answers in his mouth" (leb). Too right. When you're fully aware that the words you speak are God working through you to bless another person, that's definitely a cause for joy. Shared joy at that.

. . . and how good is . . .
Proverbs 15:23

Good is a word that's easy to discount. On a scale from *horrible* to *fabulous, good* falls somewhere in the ho-hum middle. We equate it with *okay* or *average* or *nice*. But that's not how this *good* works. Oh no. Think "wonderful" (tlb), "beautiful!" (msg), "delightful" (nasb). Think "good!" (ylt), with an exclamation point. "There is nothing better" (erv) than this kind of good; in fact, it's "always best" (wyc).

. . . a timely word! *Proverbs 15:23*

Maybe you've read a verse posted on Facebook or printed on a greeting card and thought, *That is exactly the word I needed from God today.* Yes, it is. Exactly. God offers "just the right word" (GNT) to meet our needs, to alter our thinking, to change our hearts, to shape our behavior. It comes "at the right moment" (AMP) and is "spoken in due season" (KJV).

It's also possible to blurt out an untimely word at the worst possible moment.

On a Thursday evening my daughter-in-law and I were headed to one of my speaking events, where she would be helping at our resource table for the first time. We were chatting away in the car, excited about the hours ahead. Then as we turned into the church parking lot, she made an innocent comment, which I completely misunderstood. Instead of asking her to clarify, I responded with a sharp retort even as my heart was shouting, *Don't go there, Liz!*

Too late. The words were out of my mouth, and no amount of backpedaling could repair the damage. She darted inside the church, hiding tears, while I tried to smile and greet everyone and figure out what in the world had come over me. It wasn't the Holy Spirit, I can tell you that. He gives us good words, timely words.

But the Enemy holds out words too. When we let our guard drop, when we're tired or careless or thoughtless or foolish or anxious, when we don't take time to ask questions or seek answers, we may say things we don't mean and then instantly regret them.

Yes, even in a church parking lot on a Thursday.

This story has a happy ending, though it took a sincere apology and a heartfelt conversation to fully mend our relationship. Maybe you've been there as well and are still chastising yourself for something you said long ago. Beloved, what matters now is that we learn from our mistakes. In that split second between thinking and speaking, let's put our lips on Pause, listen intently for God's clear direction, and then let Him do the talking.

Lord God,
You shower me daily
with well-timed words.
Now and again
You've even trusted me with
a timely word for someone You love.
But, Father,
when my own words are poorly timed,
when they are anything but good,
please forgive me.
Help me apologize to
those I've offended or hurt.
Trust me once more
to speak the truth in love.

His Word, Your Heart

> **Tip #28 for memorizing Scripture:**
> Find a Christian song based on
> the verse you're learning.

Proverbs 15:23 from the New International Version:

A person finds joy
in giving an apt reply—
and how good is a timely word!

Proverbs 15:23 from your favorite translation:

29

Room Service

My Father's house has many rooms;
if that were not so, would I have told you
that I am going there to prepare a place for you?

JOHN 14:2

*I*f you've always pictured God's house as an enormous estate with manicured lawns and endless hallways leading to spacious rooms, get ready for a new view of your heavenly home.

Jesus was speaking privately with His disciples, comforting and encouraging them as His crucifixion drew near. He'd already washed their feet, warned them a betrayal was imminent, and predicted Peter's denial. Now He wanted to put their minds at ease about what was to come.

"Do not let your hearts be troubled,"[1] Jesus told His followers. "Don't get lost in despair" (VOICE). To think, He was facing death on the cross, yet He was concerned about their anxious hearts! "You believe in God," He reminded them. "Believe also in me."[2]

Jesus clearly wanted to bolster their faith. So He described where they would live together someday.

My Father's house . . . *John 14:2*

We've read this phrase elsewhere in the Bible. When Jesus came to the temple in Jerusalem and found people selling cattle, sheep, and doves, as well as exchanging money, He drove them away, declaring, "Stop turning my Father's house into a market!"[3]

Now in John 14 these same words take on a greater meaning than a temple made of wood and stone. "My Father's house" is the heavenly place where the Father lives. It's also the place to which Jesus ascended after His resurrection and where the children of God will live forever.

It's His Father's house, and it's our Father's house. It's home. Not our temporary earthly home, but our permanent heavenly home. And it's *huge.*

. . . has many rooms; . . . *John 14:2*

There's "plenty of room for you" (MSG). In fact, "room to spare" (CEB). For those who've spent their days living in a crowded hovel in India or a dilapidated shack in Indonesia or a cramped trailer in Indiana, the space alone will be a luxury. "There is more than enough room in my Father's home" (NLT).

But a seventeenth-century translation rendered this word "mansions" (KJV), which started believers down the palatial path, singing, "When from the dust of death I rise / To claim my mansion in the skies."[4] Good heavens. How did we get there? Three words in three different languages pointed us in the wrong direction.

The Greek word *moné* simply means "abode." Nothing fancy, just a place to live. Then came the Latin word *mansio,* which referred to a traveler's resting place. As centuries passed, the English word *mansion* took on a grander meaning, leading to a materialistic view of heaven that Jesus never intended.

Our future lies with our Master, not our mansion. What matters is that He lives there and so will we.

> . . . if that were not so, . . . *John 14:2*

"If that weren't the case" (CEB), Jesus said, putting aside any question of it not being true, all the while speaking to their doubt and ours. I confess, I've had a few fleeting moments over the years when I questioned everything about my beliefs, including heaven. *Can it all be true? Can the Bible be trusted?*

You know the answer. I do too. But it's okay to raise questions, to ask for wisdom, to seek assurance, to wonder aloud, to examine our faith. Jesus can handle our doubts and fears. "Cast your cares on the LORD and he will sustain you; he will never let the righteous be shaken."[5]

> . . . would I have told you that . . . *John 14:2*

Jesus gently reminded them, "I would not tell you this if it were not so" (GNT). He always speaks the truth. Always. This promise is built on the infallible nature of His Word and the undeniable depth of His love.

> . . . I am going there . . . *John 14:2*

Jesus cautioned His disciples, "I am going away" (AMPC), meaning He was bound for heaven and therefore was going to die. He'd told His disciples this many times in many ways. But because they didn't want to hear it, they ignored it. Don't we do the same thing? Pretend that death doesn't exist or that it's so far in the future we don't have to think about it?

I no longer fear death, for one reason: Jesus has gone ahead of us. He has opened the door to heaven and is waiting to welcome us home.

. . . to prepare a place for you? John 14:2

Matthew Henry wrote, "Heaven would be an unready place for a Christian if Christ were not there."⁶ But He is there, getting ready for each of us. Can you imagine it? Can your mind stretch far enough to grasp that Jesus is making "arrangements for your arrival" (VOICE)?

He is thinking of you right this minute and laboring on your behalf. He knows exactly how much space will be needed. None of this "no room at the inn" talk. He is fully prepared for you and knows the hour of your arrival.

We have no such guarantees on earth. I once called ahead to a hotel in Nashville to be certain my room would be waiting for me since I wouldn't arrive until eleven at night. "Oh yes, Mrs. Higgs," the desk clerk said. "We have a room for you."

But when I showed up at the front desk an hour later, exhausted and ready for a big, comfy bed, I was told by the same clerk, "Oh no, Mrs. Higgs. We don't have a room for you."

I tried to sound professional, without a hint of whining or desperation in my voice. "Are you sure? Can you not find one little room?" He could not.

Our Savior is far more trustworthy than any hotel chain, any concierge, any front-desk clerk. Since He says He will "get a room ready for you" (MSG), you don't need to call ahead. Your room is waiting and ready. A reminder of how personal Jesus is in His care of every believer.

On earth we are strangers in a strange land. Heaven is our true home. Mansion or cabin, our dwelling place is with Him.

Lord Jesus,
it's a relief to know
my homecoming
is entirely in Your hands.
The when, where, and how
are already known to You.
All that matters to me is
knowing You will be there
to welcome me home.

His Word, Your Heart

John 14:2 from the New International Version:

My Father's house has many rooms;
if that were not so, would I have told you
that I am going there to prepare a place for you?

John 14:2 from your favorite translation:

30

Great Love

Because of the LORD's great love
we are not consumed,
for his compassions never fail.

LAMENTATIONS 3:22

It was a bright Sunday morning in south Georgia. The children's choir stood on the carpeted platform in two fidgety rows while their parents beamed. Anticipation hung in the air like dust motes.

When the piano introduction began, a fair-haired boy stepped forward to sing the call to worship. After two faltering notes he burst into tears.

A hush fell over the crowded sanctuary as his mother and the choir director both hurried to his side. They gently took the microphone from his trembling hands, then escorted him to a quiet corner out of sight from the congregation.

Sitting a few feet away, I could hear his muffled sobs. *Bless his heart.* When the choir had rehearsed a few minutes earlier, his voice had been remarkably strong and clear. Now, with the whole world watching, his confidence had plummeted.

We've all been there. Too scared to sing out, to speak up, to raise our hand, to take a chance, to offer our opinion, to say, "I can do this."

And imagine being in his mother's shoes, searching for the right words to say while two hundred people anxiously waited for the service to continue.

Whatever comfort she offered, it was effective. Moments later her young son reappeared, wiping his cheeks dry with one hand and gripping the microphone with the other. The congregation applauded. Even before they heard him sing, they honored his willingness to try.

When the boy took his place front and center, I realized what his mother must have promised him: *"I'll sing with you."* Kneeling close beside him, she wrapped her arm around his waist, leaned toward the microphone, and matched her pitch with his.

Their two voices sounded like one.

With each note he stood a little taller. Sang a little louder. When the choir joined in, his mother eased back so he could do all the arm movements to the song. But she never left his side, never stopped smiling through her tears.

This is what God does for us. He sings when we can't sing. He does what we can't do. He gives us strength. He remains by our side.

Because of the Lord's . . . *Lamentations 3:22*

Here's the Source of our hope, the Source of our strength: "It is because of" (NLV) God, and it's "through" (NKJV) God. We can't survive apart from Him. We might breathe, eat, sleep, and work, but we can't truly *live* without Him. Those of us who have tried and failed know it's only because of God that we're still here. And it's only "because of him that you are in Christ Jesus."[1]

Oh, what a gift!

His mercy is His to keep, yet He's willing to share it with us. It's His possession, yet He generously gives it away. It's the free gift "of *ADONAI*" (CJB) yet bought with a price. It's the one thing we need yet sometimes struggle to receive. Open your arms, beloved. This gift is meant for you.

. . . great love . . . *Lamentations 3:22*

This beautiful Hebrew word *chesed* is also translated "lovingkind-nesses" (ASV), "faithful love" (CEB), "steadfast love" (ESV), "unfailing love" (GNT). The kind of love only God can provide.

We use the word *love* so freely. We love our cars, our pets, a funny video we saw on YouTube. *Chesed* is another kind of love altogether. It's how God defines and demonstrates His everlasting covenant with His people.

When He faithfully blesses those who've done nothing to deserve it, that's *chesed*. When He fulfills a promise that cost Him dearly, that's *chesed*. When His Son hung on the cross for our sins, that was *chesed* in its fullest expression. How wide and long and high and deep are "the kindnesses of Jehovah!" (YLT).

. . . we . . . *Lamentations 3:22*

Though the word is always translated "we," it's worth asking who *we* refers to.

"Whoever believes in the Son."[2] That's who. "But whoever rejects the Son will not see life, for God's wrath remains on them."[3] When people list their favorite verses, they seldom choose one about God's wrath. We'd much rather hear about God's lovingkindness—and I'd much rather write about it! But God's mercy can't be fully understood apart from His wrath. Realizing that He has the power and the right to crush us yet chooses to love and forgive us makes this promise all the more amazing.

. . . are not consumed, . . . Lamentations 3:22

There's something unnerving about the word *consumed,* as if a great monster were grinding us between its teeth. The truth isn't far from it. Without God's love we would be "completely destroyed" (NIrV) and utterly "extinguished" (KNOX). Yet we are not consumed, this verse assures us. We are "still alive" (ERV).

. . . for his compassions . . . Lamentations 3:22

"His mercies" (ESV) are plural, multiple. Not a one-time thing, but an endless outpouring, for which I am beyond grateful. Every time I go to the Lord begging His forgiveness for the same failings, the same stupidities, the same sins, I almost hold my breath, fearing His voice will thunder from the heavens, "Enough, Liz! I don't want to hear it."

But that's not what He says. Not the God of *chesed.* His "commiserations" (DRA), His "merciful doings" (WYC) flow over all of us who depend on His kindness.

Years ago when I was trying to help our son with his homework, he was getting more discouraged by the minute. Finally I asked him, "Do you know why I'm pushing so hard?"

Matt's little shoulders drooped. "Because you want me to get a good grade."

"No, sweetie." I hugged him and then whispered into the curve of his ear, "Because I love you."

That's what God is saying to you as well, dear friend. He doesn't care about your performance. He cares about you.

God sayed the best and most encouraging words for last.

. . . never fail. *Lamentations 3:22*

Those mercies, that fountain of grace, will "never cease" (NLT). *Never* is a word that leaves no room for discussion. No room for fear either. God's lovingkindness "never ends" (NLV), and He is "never weary" (KNOX). God keeps reminding us of this, hoping we'll finally grasp the reality of it: "Love never fails."[4]

This day, this hour, when His mercies are new once again, may His truth wash over you afresh: you are loved.

Father God,
Your love never ceases
to amaze me.
The breadth and depth
of Your grace,
the boundless, endless supply
of Your mercy
are gifts beyond imagining.
I need You, Lord.
And I would not dream of living
without You.

His Word, Your Heart

Tip #30 for memorizing Scripture:
Teach the verse to others.

Lamentations 3:22 from the New International Version:
Because of the LORD's great love
we are not consumed,
for his compassions never fail.

Lamentations 3:22 from your favorite translation:

31

Lean on Me

Trust in the LORD with all your heart
and lean not on your own understanding.

PROVERBS 3:5

*T*rust. Out of sheer necessity it's the first thing a child learns. When the room is cold, she soon discovers she has not been forgotten. A blanket appears. When he cries for food, he quickly realizes he has been heard. A breast, a bottle, a spoon touches his tiny mouth.

Sadly, if children's basic needs aren't met, trust in others often eludes them right into adulthood.

As a young woman I had a knack for giving my heart to people who were untrustworthy, who said one thing yet did another, who could smile and lie without blinking an eye.

In my naiveté I believed that love and trust were one and the same. I didn't understand that regardless of how quickly I fell in love, learning to trust that person was another matter. Trust required a season of testing and waiting, of promises kept and expectations met.

I was too impatient for all that. My once-tender heart was soon bruised, wounded, broken, hardened until I was wary of loving anyone. Then God appeared. Or rather, my eyes were opened, since He was always there and is now and always will be. And here is what I read in His Word: "Love the LORD your God with all your heart."[1] "Trust in the LORD with all your heart."[2] "Obey from your heart the pattern of teaching that has now claimed your allegiance."[3] Love. Trust. Obey. God wanted it all.

Loving Him came easily once I grasped the magnitude of His love for His children. But trusting Him completely? The whole "Let go, let God" thing? That took years. And obedience? Oh my, oh my. A work in progress.

That's why God must teach His children as if we were newborns frightened by loud sounds and confused by our surroundings. We need to learn a new language called *grace* and a new way of living called *loved* so we can trust Him with our whole hearts.

Years ago while I was busily organizing our wedding, my sweet Bill was quietly planning our honeymoon. Whenever I asked him what he had in mind, Bill just smiled and said, "You'll love it." I had confidence in him because I adored him and because he'd already proven himself trustworthy. Not knowing the details of where we were going was part of the adventure.

On a much grander scale, that's what God is saying to us: "Trust me. You will love the plans I've made for you." Because God is writing your story, you can be sure it will end on just the right note: "And she lived happily ever after."

What He asks of us, though, isn't a baby step. It's a huge leap of faith.

Trust in the LORD with all your heart . . . *Proverbs 3:5*

He calls us to "lean on, trust in, and be confident" (AMPC) in Him. Not to second-guess our commitment to Him. Not to look over our shoulders and wonder what we might be missing.

In order to "place your trust" (VOICE) in God, you must first lift some things off your shoulders—the need for control, the need to have all the answers—and deposit them into His loving hands.

Then you must let go.

I know. *So* hard.

In Hebrew *kol* means "all." Not some, not most, but all. Holding nothing back, making no demands, we must "completely" (ERV) release our deep need to be in charge. The Lord knows how hard this is for us and what it will cost us to trust Him. The sacrifice of self. The putting aside of pride. The laying down of arms.

No more fighting Him. No more insistence on having our own way. As if we knew best. As if.

. . . and lean not on your own understanding. *Proverbs 3:5*

It's helpful to have something to lean on. A rail when we climb steps. The back of a chair when we have to pull on a shoe. But "lean not" isn't asking us to avoid a physical action. "Lean not" means "don't depend" (ERV) and "do not rely" (AMP) on that which is undependable and unreliable.

The Hebrew word *shaan* means "to lean, to support oneself." When you think about it, leaning on or supporting yourself is nigh to impossible. Where would you put your hand? Where would you rest your weight?

The One who loves us knows we can't stand on our own. Depend wholly on ourselves? Go through life without Him? We're simply not built to do that. Whether we call it "insight" (AMP) or "intelligence" (CEB) or "judgment" (CEV), our own understanding is not to be trusted. "What you think you know" (GNT) isn't enough to carry you through.

Our flawed thinking will invariably lead us downward rather than upward. The Lord who formed our gray matter and shaped our intellect cautions us, "Never depend upon your own ideas and inventions" (VOICE),

"The knowing"

and whatever you do, "don't try to figure out everything on your own" (MSG).

His Word assures us "the works of his hands are faithful and just; all his precepts are trustworthy."[4] Because God knows us well, He shows us well. He demonstrates His trustworthiness again and again in our lives.

Then our trust in Him becomes more than a shrug, an acknowledgment, an "I guess so." It's a trust grounded in experiences we can point to. "Look! God did this for me," and "No one but the Lord could have managed this," and "See? He came through at just the right time!"

Remembering those moments in your life when God stepped in can build and strengthen your faith. Whether He spares you from tragedy or walks you through it, this is a God you can trust.

It's time, my friend. Are you ready? Can you let go of everything? And trust God for anything?

Lord, I want to trust You in all things,
not just some things.
Help me learn from You.
Help me lean on You.
Help me let go of my stubborn need to control.
Help me understand that loving You
with all my heart means
trusting You
with all I was and am and will be.
Thank You, Jesus,
for never tiring of showing me
how truly trustworthy You are.

His Word, Your Heart

Tip #31 for memorizing Scripture:

Continue reviewing verses
once you've memorized them.
It's the key to storing them in our
hearts with absolute accuracy.

Proverbs 3:5 from the New International Version:

Trust in the Lord with all your heart
and lean not on your own understanding.

Proverbs 3:5 from your favorite translation:

WRITE THESE
31 Verses on Your Heart

*Fix these words of mine
in your hearts and minds.*

DEUTERONOMY 11:18

*N*ow that we've studied (word for word for word!) our thirty-one verses, let's make every effort to commit them to memory—not for a month, but for a lifetime. When the Lord prepared Joshua for his new leadership role, He commanded him, "Keep this Book of the Law always on your lips; meditate on it day and night."[1] That's been our goal since page one.

Here are all our memorization tips, gathered in one list. Feel free to skip over any that don't work for you—except the first one.

1. **Pray.** It's the most important step of all. None of us can do this on our own.

2. **Memorize the reference, then the verse, and then repeat the reference.** Since the book name and the chapter and verse numbers are the hardest bits to remember, put that information first and last.

3. **Pick a good place.** It helps to do memory work in consistent surroundings.

4. **Choose the best time of day, when your mind is at its sharpest.** That's your ideal time for memory work.

5. **Set an alarm to remind you to review your verse.** A memory jogger helps us be accountable.

6. **Decide on the best translation for you.** I love to read the New Living Translation and to study the New International Version, but when it comes to memorization, I prefer the New American Standard Bible, in part because the phrasing is so musical and therefore easier to remember, and the translation is highly respected.

7. **Learn one verse at a time.** I have friends who tackle long passages, full chapters, even whole books of the Bible. Impressive. Still, it all begins with one verse.

8. **Start with one verse a week.** It's a modest goal. But if we learn just one a week, that's fifty verses a year (with a little vacation time thrown in).

9. **Begin with the shortest, most personally meaningful verses, and grow from there.** After all, the Bible Memorization Police won't be stopping by your house. You can also break longer verses into segments and put them together as you go.

10. **Say the verse aloud.** The best way to make the words stick is to recite them, even if the Lord is the only One listening.

11. **Stand up and walk around to stay energized and focused.** Scientists who study the brain can explain how and why this

works. I just know that movement helps me remember what I'm learning.

12. **Use gestures with each word to emphasize and illustrate the verse.** Again, this helps with retention.

13. **Record the verse on your phone or a digital recorder.** Listening to a verse is a great way to review it when you're on the road.

14. **Write the verse across a sheet of paper.** Some of us learn best by speaking words, others by writing them. It's wise to do both.

15. **Once you've written the verse, underline or highlight the key words.** Get creative. Use different color pens. The idea is to capture not only the words themselves but also the gist of the verse.

16. **Write and rewrite the verse as many times as you can fit it on a sheet of paper.** Repetition is our friend. Now turn the paper over and write the verse from memory.

17. **Draw a picture to illustrate the verse you're memorizing.** Stick figures are fine. The idea is to create a unique image for each verse. If it's laughable, so much the better—it will also be more memorable.

18. **Try journaling while you study God's Word. Or explore a creative approach such as *verse mapping*.** Proverbs31.org offers a free online resource.[2]

19. **Find a photo that suits the verse, creating another way to jog your memory.** This is especially helpful for those of us who have no artistic ability whatsoever. Print the photos, collect them in a computer file, or organize them on Pinterest.com for easy reference.

20. **Sing the verse to the tune of a familiar song. Or create a simple rhythm you can tap out.** Even if you're not musical, both methods will help the words find a nesting place in your heart.

21. **Make it personal.** Mine your memory for a life experience that illustrates the verse.

22. **Include the verse in your prayers.** The Lord loves to hear His Word, especially when it flows in a natural and meaningful way during your private conversations with Him.

23. **Add the verse below your signature on e-mails and letters.** This provides more ways to incorporate Scripture into your life, to keep it foremost in your mind, and to share your love for the Lord with others.

24. **Post the verse on social media.** We all need as much wisdom as we can get!

25. **Put the verse where you'll see it daily—the more locations, the better.** Place it on a bulletin board, mirror, fridge, car dashboard, or computer screen, where it will easily catch your eye.

26. **Carry the verse in your purse for easy review.** It's a great use of time when you get stuck in traffic or in a long line at the grocery store.

27. **Write the verse on a flashcard,** put the reference on the flip side, and then have others test you.

28. **Find a Christian song based on the verse you're learning.** Classic hymns and the best of our modern worship songs often incorporate God's Word and provide another way to commit a verse to heart.

29. **Practice the verse while you're walking, gardening, cleaning, exercising, bathing, dressing—**anytime your mind is free to focus on God's life-changing Word.

30. **Teach the verse to others.** One-on-one, around the table with your family or in a classroom setting, explain what the verse means in context and what it means to you.

31. **Continue reviewing verses once you've memorized them.**
It's the key to storing them in our hearts with absolute accuracy.

Consider these as merely suggestions. Embrace, adapt, or ignore them as you wish. I'm so proud of you for giving Scripture memorization a try. Let me know how you're doing. I'm cheering for you!

Study Guide

*I*f you're ready to consider the timeless truths you've learned from these verses and apply them to your twenty-first-century life, this Study Guide was designed for you. Whether used on your own or in a small-group setting, these questions will help you delve deeper into Scripture for a richer and more satisfying takeaway.

You'll need a place to record your answers—tablet, notebook, computer, whatever you choose—plus an open Bible and an open heart. God meets with us when we gather around His Word, and He often surprises us with fresh discoveries about our relationship with Him.

VERSE 1: WRITE ON, SISTER

Let love and faithfulness never leave you;
bind them around your neck,
write them on the tablet of your heart. PROVERBS 3:3

1. What is a Bible verse you especially like? Why is it meaningful to you?

2. God's love and faithfulness truly are inseparable. In what ways do Psalms 26:3; 36:5; 40:11; 85:10; and 89:14 reinforce that truth? And why do those two qualities go hand in hand?

 ## Verse 2: All New You

Therefore, if anyone is in Christ, the new creation has come: The old has gone, the new is here! 2 Corinthians 5:17

1. Was there a defining moment when you became a follower of Christ? If you can't pinpoint a date and time, how do you know without a doubt that vital change took place? What assurance might Ephesians 2:8–10 offer?

2. Just as 2 Corinthians 5:17 begins with "therefore," so does Romans 8:1. Read Romans 7:21–25 for a bit of background. Then consider each word and phrase in Romans 8:1, noting what it reveals about this foundational truth for believers and how that truth encourages you.

> Therefore:
> there is now:
> no condemnation:
> for those who are in Christ Jesus:

Verse 3: Afraid Not

Fear of man will prove to be a snare,
but whoever trusts in the LORD is kept safe. Proverbs 29:25

1. Hebrews 13:6 boldly asks, "What can mere mortals do to me?" How would you respond to that question in light of your life experiences?

2. If you're prone to worry about people's opinions of you, what might help you rest in God's opinion? Or if you have no fear of what people think, what helped you achieve that mind-set?

🌹 VERSE 4: GREAT EXPECTATIONS

"For I know the plans I have for you," declares the LORD, "plans to prosper you and not to harm you, plans to give you hope and a future."
JEREMIAH 29:11

1. When I asked one thousand women to name their favorite verse, Jeremiah 29:11 won by a landslide. How has this verse comforted or encouraged you in the past?

2. Now that you know the difficult context in which these words were written, how might this verse strengthen your faith in the future? What additional insight does Proverbs 24:14 offer?

🌹 VERSE 5: START SMART

The fear of the LORD is the beginning of wisdom, and knowledge of the Holy One is understanding. PROVERBS 9:10

1. Psalm 96:4 reminds us, "For great is the LORD and most worthy of praise; he is to be feared above all gods." What does *fearing God* mean to you?

2. God reminds us in Isaiah 55:9, "As the heavens are higher than the earth, so are my ways higher than your ways and my thoughts than your thoughts." Since He is beyond us in every possible way yet calls us to *know* Him, what might "knowing Him" mean?

Verse 6: Can Do

I can do all this through him who gives me strength. Philippians 4:13

1. If you are an I-can-do-this kind of person, how has your approach to challenges hindered or helped your walk with Christ?

2. If you are more reticent in nature, what do you need strength for right now in your life? Whatever your personality, how might the truth of this verse and Psalm 105:4 help you move forward?

 ## Verse 7: Safe Guard

Above all else, guard your heart,
for everything you do flows from it. Proverbs 4:23

1. Practically speaking, what can you do to guard your heart and keep it pure? What hedges do you need to build around it? And to what earthly protectors might you turn?

2. Read Psalm 51:10 and Matthew 5:8. How can an unclean heart be made clean again? What promise is given to those whose hearts are pure?

 ## Verse 8: Blown Away

For the Spirit God gave us does not make us timid, but gives us power,
love and self-discipline. 2 Timothy 1:7

1. In this chapter I shared an embarrassing incident when I was anything but timid and exerted the wrong kind of power. Perhaps you've had a similar experience. What did you learn from it?

2. Galatians 5:22–23 shows us what sweet fruit we bear when we're filled with the Holy Spirit. As you consider that list, which spiritual qualities have ripened in you? And which ones have yet to bud? What, if anything, do you need to do to promote growth, or do you simply need to trust the Lord's timing? What makes you say that?

 ## VERSE 9: GOD WORKS

And we know that in all things God works for the good of those who love him, who have been called according to his purpose.
ROMANS 8:28

1. Too often this wonderful verse has been misquoted or misunderstood. What new insight did God reveal to you as we studied Romans 8:28 together?

2. Philippians 2:13 further describes how God works, most clearly in this translation: "For God is working in you, giving you the desire and the power to do what pleases him" (NLT). We know we're not puppets in His hands. How then does He give us the *desire* and the *power* to do His will?

 ## VERSE 10: CHARM SCHOOL

Charm is deceptive, and beauty is fleeting;
but a woman who fears the LORD is to be praised. PROVERBS 31:30

1. Can charm or beauty ever be used for a good purpose? If not, why? If so, when? Does a woman need either charm or beauty to serve the Lord? What brought you to that conclusion?

2. We seldom hear the phrase "God-fearing people" anymore, yet what do Proverbs 1:7 and 9:10 tell us? If you are "a woman who fears the LORD," what does that look like in your daily life?

 ### VERSE 11: JUST STOP

He says, "Be still, and know that I am God;
I will be exalted among the nations,
I will be exalted in the earth." PSALM 46:10

1. Now that we know "be still" really means stop fighting and cease striving, what is God asking you to be still about this week?

2. Write out Psalm 116:7. What does this word from His Word say to you right now?

 ### VERSE 12: LOVE SONG

The LORD your God is with you,
the Mighty Warrior who saves.
He will take great delight in you;
in his love he will no longer rebuke you,
but will rejoice over you with singing. ZEPHANIAH 3:17

1. Usually we are the ones singing to the Lord. See Psalm 98:4–6. Does the thought of the Lord singing over you make you smile? Tremble? Weep? What words would you most want to hear Him sing?

2. Psalm 32:7 also speaks of God surrounding us with music. Describe how you imagine those songs would sound. What makes music such a powerful means of expression?

Verse 13: All Grown Up

Start children off on the way they should go,
and even when they are old they will not turn from it. Proverbs 22:6

1. If you're a parent, what comfort or encouragement does this verse offer you? How would you define "the way they should go"?

2. If you don't have children, what hope do you find in this verse regarding the next generation? What assurance about the church does Ephesians 3:21 offer?

Verse 14: Comfort Food

So do not fear, for I am with you;
do not be dismayed, for I am your God.
I will strengthen you and help you;
I will uphold you with my righteous right hand. Isaiah 41:10

1. Do you have a deep-seated fear in your life or a weakness you can't seem to overcome? What hope do the promises in this verse offer you? How do you experience God's presence in those difficult moments?

2. Many passages in Scripture speak of the power of God's right hand. Read Exodus 15:6; Psalm 16:11; and Acts 7:55, and note any discoveries you find.

Verse 15: Fret Not

Do not be anxious about anything, but in every situation, by prayer and
petition, with thanksgiving, present your requests to God. Philippians 4:6

1. In this chapter I mentioned a "huge thing pressing on your heart 24/7." Now put that concern into words. How might Matthew 11:28–30 help lessen your anxiety?

2. What will it take for you to gift-wrap that situation and completely give it to God, knowing it will be in very good hands? Whom might you ask to pray for you in this process?

🌹 Verse 16: It's Tough to Be Gentle

A gentle answer turns away wrath,
but a harsh word stirs up anger. Proverbs 15:1

1. This two-part verse gives us a contrast to consider. Which is your natural bent—to be gentle when you speak or to be harsh? When have you seen gentleness ease a tense situation?

2. What ideas do you find in 1 Corinthians 4:21 and Ephesians 4:2 that can help you put this proverb into practice?

🌹 Verse 17: This Is It

Give thanks in all circumstances; for this is God's will for you in Christ Jesus. 1 Thessalonians 5:18

1. Describe a time when you were able to give thanks to God in a difficult circumstance. How did it help you? And how did others respond? If you've not been able to do that, how can you remind yourself to praise God no matter what is going on in your life?

2. Write out Psalm 7:17 and Psalm 106:1. If you've chosen to memorize Scripture, these two verses are ideal. What does each of them teach you about why we're to give thanks to God?

VERSE 18: LOVELY THOUGHTS

Finally, brothers and sisters, whatever is true, whatever is noble, whatever is right, whatever is pure, whatever is lovely, whatever is admirable—if anything is excellent or praiseworthy—think about such things. PHILIPPIANS 4:8

1. If you can, describe a time when you sensed the Holy Spirit guarding and guiding your thoughts, keeping your mind from going in the wrong direction.

2. If focusing on what is excellent and praiseworthy is a challenge for you, what are some practical solutions for this spiritual struggle? For all the times you stumble, what remedy do you find in Hebrews 10:22?

VERSE 19: LAUGHING MATTERS

She is clothed with strength and dignity; she can laugh at the days to come. PROVERBS 31:25

1. The happiest families have private jokes and inside humor that they revisit. Describe something funny that happened in your childhood or in your current household. Why does that memory still tickle you?

2. Laughing at the past is one thing. This verse calls us to laugh at the future. What advice does Psalm 37:37 offer for preparing yourself for the months and years ahead?

 ## Verse 20: High Flying

But those who hope in the LORD
will renew their strength.
They will soar on wings like eagles;
they will run and not grow weary,
they will walk and not be faint. Isaiah 40:31

1. In what areas of your life do you feel weary or weak? What comfort do you find in Isaiah 40:29?

2. What could you do differently, starting this very day, to put your hope more fully in the Lord and truly soar like an eagle?

 ## Verse 21: Sharp Edge, Clean Cut

As iron sharpens iron,
so one person sharpens another. Proverbs 27:17

1. What other believer has sharpened your faith, and how did he or she do so?

2. Ecclesiastes 4:9–10 describes some of the benefits of doing life with others who love God. What does this passage say to you?

Verse 22: Perfect Peace

You will keep in perfect peace
those whose minds are steadfast,
because they trust in you. Isaiah 26:3

1. What is perfect peace? What would it look like or feel like to you?

2. During His earthly ministry Jesus was not only a peacemaker; He was also a peace giver. Read Luke 7:50 and Luke 8:48, and note what Jesus said and did to give these women peace. Where is Jesus telling you to "go in peace" today, trusting Him with the outcome?

 ## Verse 23: Start to Finish

Being confident of this, that he who began a good work in you will carry it on to completion until the day of Christ Jesus. Philippians 1:6

1. Paul was confident that God will continue His good work in those He loves. What evidence have you seen in your life that God is still watering, pruning, fertilizing?

2. What truth in 1 Corinthians 1:8 further assures you that God is still working in and through your life?

 ## Verse 24: With You

Have I not commanded you? Be strong and courageous. Do not be afraid; do not be discouraged, for the LORD your God will be with you wherever you go. Joshua 1:9

1. In what area(s) of your life do you particularly need God's strength and courage? If something strikes fear in your heart or weighs heavily on your shoulders right now, how could you start entrusting it to God?

2. Read Genesis 26:24 and 28:15. When you believe that God is always with you, what specific differences does it make in the way you handle each day?

VERSE 25: FLAWLESS

Every word of God is flawless;
he is a shield to those who take refuge in him. PROVERBS 30:5

1. What does Psalm 12:6 say about the purity of God's Word? Do a little research on the processes involved in refining silver and gold. What parallels do you see to the way God's Word refines you?

2. Read Psalm 18:2. Now draw a shield (no one has to see it!), and then write across that shield all the attributes the psalmist recognizes in God. This shield—this God—goes before you. How can you remind yourself of this truth daily so you feel more secure?

VERSE 26: LOVE MERCY

He has shown you, O mortal, what is good.
And what does the LORD require of you?
To act justly and to love mercy
and to walk humbly with your God. MICAH 6:8

1. Humility comes from seeing ourselves for what we truly are
(broken, sinful, needy) and recognizing God for who He truly is
(powerful, loving, merciful). Describe the most humble person you
know. What aspects of that person's behavior will you ask God to
nurture in you?

2. Of the three things God requires of His people in this verse—act
justly, love mercy, walk humbly—which one is the hardest for you?
In order to grow in that particular area, what changes will you ask
the Holy Spirit to make in you?

 VERSE 27: FEARLESS

But now, this is what the LORD says—
he who created you, Jacob,
he who formed you, Israel:
"Do not fear, for I have redeemed you;
I have summoned you by name; you are mine." ISAIAH 43:1

1. How does each of these four assurances from God speak to you,
and why?

> Do not fear:
> For I have redeemed you:
> I have summoned you by name:
> You are mine:

2. You'll find further assurance in 1 John 3:1. Note what you discover
in that verse that is especially comforting to you right now.

Verse 28: Right Answer

A person finds joy in giving an apt reply—
and how good is a timely word! Proverbs 15:23

1. If God has ever offered someone a timely word through you,
   describe what happened. What was that person's reaction? And
   how did that experience affect you?

2. What advice for being ready to share a good and helpful word do
   you find in 1 Peter 3:15? And what counsel for avoiding the wrong
   words does Ephesians 4:25 offer?

 ### Verse 29: Room Service

My Father's house has many rooms; if that were not so, would
I have told you that I am going there to prepare a place for you?
John 14:2

1. If you've always pictured yourself living in a grand heavenly
   mansion, what is your response to the biblical truth that heaven is
   simply living with Jesus?

2. What do Ecclesiastes 3:11 and John 6:40 reveal about eternity?
   And what single word would you use to describe heaven?

 ### Verse 30: Great Love

Because of the Lord's great love we are not consumed,
for his compassions never fail. Lamentations 3:22

1. If you've ever clung to the truth of this verse during a time you sorely needed God's compassion, what did you learn through the process?

2. Read Psalms 86:15; 103:13; and 145:9. What picture do they paint of God's lovingkindness? What are some ways you could reflect His compassion in your interactions with others?

 ## Verse 31: Lean on Me

Trust in the LORD with all your heart
and lean not on your own understanding. Proverbs 3:5

1. Which half of this verse is the most challenging for you— depending wholly on God or no longer depending on yourself? Why might that be the case?

2. Read the following verses about God's trustworthiness: Psalms 9:10; 28:7; and 112:7. What other examples can you find in Scripture? Now finish this statement in your own words: "I can trust in the Lord with all my heart because _____."

May the Lord richly bless the time we've spent together in His Word!

Heartfelt Thanks

First, I'm grateful for *you,* dear sister—for reading my books, for telling your friends about them, for giving them as gifts, for sharing my studies at your churches, for posting reviews online, for following my online Bible study, for sending words of encouragement. You are always on my mind and in my heart as my fingers fly across the keyboard. I hope you found the hug I tucked inside these pages.

And my editorial team? Best on the planet. Laura Barker, Carol Bartley, Sara Fortenberry, Rebecca Price, Glenna Salsbury, and Matthew Higgs—your gentle direction and enthusiastic support made the editing process painless, even fun. To Beth Higgs, my personal assistant, and Lilly Higgs, my social media maven, huge thanks for setting me free to write. As for my sweet husband, Bill Higgs, you are so right: it *does* take two people to do Lizzie. I am beyond grateful that you are the other half of this team and have been for thirty years.

Finally, kudos to my copyeditor, Lisa Guest, to Rose Decaen for her fine proofreading, to Angie Messinger for her superior typesetting skills, to Cara Iverson for proofing our final pages, to Karen Sherry for a beauti-fully designed interior, and to Kelly Howard for a book jacket that's thirty-one flavors of lovely. Though we've yet to meet, friends, I hold your finished work in my hands with deep gratitude.

Notes

Well Versed

1. John 1:1
2. John 1:1, ERV
3. John 1:1
4. Psalm 130:5
5. Deuteronomy 30:14
6. 2 Timothy 3:16
7. Proverbs 7:1
8. Proverbs 4:4
9. Psalm 119:11
10. Deuteronomy 6:7
11. Deuteronomy 6:6

1. Write On, Sister

1. Further information on the Hebrew and Greek words referenced in this book can be found in Francis Brown, S. R. Driver, and Charles A. Briggs, *The New Brown-Driver-Briggs-Gesenius Hebrew and English Lexicon* (Lafayette, IN: Associated Publishers and Authors, 1980), and Robert L. Thomas, ed., *New American Standard Exhaustive Concordance of the Bible with Hebrew-Aramaic and Greek Dictionaries* (Nashville: Holman Bible, 1981).
2. Exodus 31:18
3. Psalm 19:14

2. All New You

1. Matthew 17:20
2. John 4:10
3. John 15:5
4. Matthew 16:15–17
5. Acts 17:28
6. Romans 6:23
7. Romans 8:1
8. Philippians 1:6

3. Afraid Not

1. Matthew 25:21
2. Galatians 1:10
3. Psalm 52:8
4. Psalm 56:11
5. Psalm 91:2
6. Psalm 121:7
7. Romans 8:31

4. Great Expectations

1. Kenneth Barker, ed., *The NIV Study Bible, New International Version* (Grand Rapids: Zondervan, 1985), note on Jeremiah 1:3.
2. Psalm 90:10
3. Matthew Henry, *Matthew Henry's Commentary on the Whole Bible* (Peabody, MA: Hendrickson, 1991), 4:462.
4. 1 Samuel 2:3

5. Henry, *Matthew Henry's
   Commentary,* 4:463.
6. Psalm 94:11
7. 2 Timothy 2:19
8. Ecclesiastes 3:11
9. 1 John 2:25

5. Start Smart
1. Psalm 34:11
2. Psalm 19:9
3. Joshua 24:14
4. Psalm 90:11
5. Hebrews 12:9
6. Romans 8:15
7. Lamentations 3:23, NLT
8. Job 38:4
9. Psalm 36:1

6. Can Do
1. Gwen Sharp, "Myth-Making and
   the 'We Can Do It!' Poster,"
   Sociological Images, January 4,
   2011, http://thesocietypages
   .org/socimages/2011/01/04
   /myth-making-and-the-we
   -can-do-it-poster/.
2. Ellen Fried, "From Pearl Harbor
   to Elvis: Images That Endure,"
   National Archives *Prologue
   Magazine* 36, no. 4 (Winter
   2004), www.archives.gov
   /publications/prologue/2004
   /winter/top-images.html.
3. Philippians 4:11
4. Philippians 4:12

7. Safe Guard
1. John 17:18

2. Job 22:22
3. Deuteronomy 6:5
4. Proverbs 3:5

8. Blown Away
1. Ephesians 1:13
2. Romans 5:5
3. 2 Corinthians 4:7

9. God Works
1. 1 Corinthians 10:13
2. Psalm 119:28
3. Psalm 18:32
4. Isaiah 64:8
5. Isaiah 45:9

10. Charm School
1. Proverbs 31:28
2. Annie Chapman and Maureen
   Rank, *Simplify Your Hectic Life*
   (Ada, MI: Revell, 2005), 13.
3. Job 29:2–3

11. Just Stop
1. Matthew Henry, *Matthew
   Henry's Commentary on the
   Whole Bible* (Peabody, MA:
   Hendrickson, 1991), 3:334.
2. Psalm 100:3
3. Deuteronomy 4:35
4. Philippians 2:10–11
5. Exodus 15:11
6. Genesis 1:10
7. Genesis 1:31

12. Love Song
1. Matthew Henry, *Matthew
   Henry's Commentary on the*

Whole Bible (Peabody, MA: Hendrickson, 1991), 4:1092.

13. All Grown Up

1. Proverbs 2:9
2. John 10:28
3. 2 Timothy 2:19
4. Isaiah 59:1

14. Comfort Food

1. Isaiah 41:9
2. 2 Corinthians 12:10
3. Exodus 15:6
4. Psalm 16:11
5. Psalm 89:13

15. Fret Not

1. Romans 8:26
2. Philippians 4:7

16. It's Tough to Be Gentle

1. Colossians 3:12
2. Luke 6:29
3. Ephesians 3:18

17. This Is It

1. Ecclesiastes 7:14
2. Psalm 33:4
3. Colossians 3:15

18. Lovely Thoughts

1. Psalm 119:160
2. Tallulah Bankhead, *Tallulah: My Autobiography* (Jackson, MS: University Press of Mississippi, 2004), 74.
3. 1 John 1:9
4. Ephesians 4:23

19. Laughing Matters

1. Psalm 28:7
2. Leviticus 21:8
3. Job 8:21
4. Isaiah 62:5

20. High Flying

1. Emily Dickinson, *The Complete Poems of Emily Dickinson,* ed. Thomas H. Johnson (Boston: Little, Brown, 1960), 114.
2. Psalm 91:4

21. Sharp Edge, Clean Cut

1. Hebrews 4:12
2. Psalm 64:3
3. Matthew Henry, *Matthew Henry's Commentary on the Whole Bible* (Peabody, MA: Hendrickson, 1991), 3:781.
4. Proverbs 27:6

22. Perfect Peace

1. Isaiah 26:1
2. Ecclesiastes 3:14
3. Isaiah 49:16
4. 2 Samuel 22:31
5. Isaiah 57:19
6. Philippians 4:7
7. Acts 22:14
8. Proverbs 16:9, CEV
9. Colossians 3:2
10. Psalm 22:5

23. Start to Finish

1. Philippians 1:3–5
2. Philippians 1:4, CEV
3. Philippians 1:5, ASV

4. Philippians 1:5, CJB
5. Philippians 1:5, OJB

24. *With You*
1. Ruth 1:16, KJV

25. *Flawless*
1. Isaiah 41:13
2. Deuteronomy 31:6
3. John 16:32
4. Psalm 9:10, CEB
5. Isaiah 43:4

26. *Love Mercy*
1. Micah 1:1
2. Micah 6:2
3. Micah 6:16
4. Job 33:12
5. Job 14:1
6. Job 15:16
7. Job 25:6
8. Psalm 90:3
9. Psalm 103:15–16
10. Mark 10:18
11. Isaiah 66:2
12. Ephesians 4:6
13. Micah 7:19

27. *Fearless*
1. Isaiah 42:20
2. Isaiah 42:18
3. Romans 11:11–24
4. Genesis 25:26
5. Genesis 28:15
6. Genesis 32:28

29. *Room Service*
1. John 14:1
2. John 14:1
3. John 2:16
4. Nikolaus L. von Zinzendorf, "Jesus, Thy Blood and Righteousness," Cyber Hymnal.org, http://cyberhymnal.org/htm/j/t/jtbloodr.htm.
5. Psalm 55:22
6. Matthew Henry, *Matthew Henry's Commentary on the Whole Bible* (Peabody, MA: Hendrickson, 1991), 5:895.

30. *Great Love*
1. 1 Corinthians 1:30
2. John 3:36
3. John 3:36
4. 1 Corinthians 13:8

31. *Lean on Me*
1. Deuteronomy 6:5
2. Proverbs 3:5
3. Romans 6:17
4. Psalm 111:7

Write These 31 Verses on Your Heart
1. Joshua 1:8
2. Proverbs 31 Ministries, Online Bible Studies, http://s3.amazonaws.com/p31obs/KIS/Verse+Mapping+-+OBS+PDF.pdf.

Additional Bible Versions

Scripture quotations marked (ASV) are taken from the American Standard Version. Scripture quotations marked (AMP) are taken from the Amplified Bible. Copyright © 2015 by the Lockman Foundation. Used by permission. (www.Lockman.org). Scripture quotations marked (AMPC) are taken from the Amplified Bible, Classic Edition. Copyright © 1954, 1958, 1962, 1964, 1965, 1987 by the Lockman Foundation. Used by permission. (www.Lockman.org). Scripture quotations marked (CEB) are taken from the Common English Bible. Copyright © 2011. Scripture quotations marked (CJB) are taken from the Complete Jewish Bible. Copyright © 1998 by David H. Stern. All rights reserved. Scripture quotations marked (CEV) are taken from the Contemporary English Version. Copyright © 1991, 1992, 1995 by American Bible Society. Used by permission. Scripture quotations marked (DRA) are taken from the Douay-Rheims 1899 American Edition. Scripture quotations marked (ERV) are taken from the Holy Bible: Easy-to-Read Version © 2014 by Bible League International. Used by permission. Scripture quotations marked (ESV) are taken from the ESV® Bible (the Holy Bible, English Standard Version®), copyright © 2001 by Crossway, a publishing ministry of Good News Publishers. Used by permission. All rights reserved. Scripture quotations marked (EXB) are taken from the Expanded Bible. Copyright © 2011 by Thomas Nelson. Used by permission. All rights reserved. Scripture quotations marked (GNV) are taken from the Geneva Bible, 1599 Edition. Published by Tolle Lege Press. All rights reserved. Scripture quotations marked (GNT) are taken from the Good News Translation in Today's English Version—Second Edition. Copyright © 1992 by American Bible Society. Used by permission. Scripture quotations marked (HCSB)

About the Author

Liz Curtis Higgs is the author of more than thirty books, with 4.6 million copies in print. In her best-selling Bad Girls of the Bible series, Liz breathes new life into ancient tales about the most famous women in scriptural history, from Bathsheba to Mary Magdalene.

In *The Girl's Still Got It,* Liz offers a twenty-first-century take on the book of Ruth, dishing out meat and milk, substance and style, in this deeply personal journey with Naomi and Ruth. *The Women of Christmas* invites readers to experience the season afresh with Elizabeth, Mary, and Anna. And in *It's Good to Be Queen,* Liz escorts readers inside the courts of King Solomon, where the queen of Sheba shows her modern sisters how to be bold, gracious, and wise.

A seasoned professional speaker and Bible study teacher, Liz has toured with Women of Faith, Women of Joy, and Extraordinary Women. She has spoken for seventeen hundred other women's conferences, which has taken her to all fifty states in the United States and fifteen foreign countries, including Thailand, Portugal, South Africa, and New Zealand.

On the personal side, Liz is married to Bill Higgs, PhD, who serves as director of operations for her speaking and writing office. Louisville, Kentucky, is home for Liz and Bill, their grown children, and their twin tabby cats, Boaz and Samson.

Follow Liz's free online Bible study on www.LizCurtisHiggs.com, and find her on www.Facebook.com/LizCurtisHiggs, on www.Twitter.com/LizCurtisHiggs, on www.Instagram.com/LizCurtisHiggs, on www.Vimeo.com/LizCurtisHiggs, and on www.Pinterest.com/LizCurtisHiggs.

LEARN THE TRUTH
ABOUT GOD'S GOODNESS FROM THE BIBLE'S BAD GIRLS

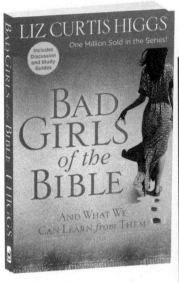
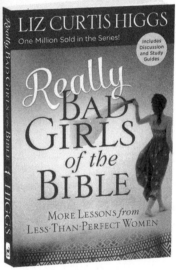

One million readers have taken a walk on the wild side with Former Bad Girl, Liz Curtis Higgs, and her eye-opening blend of contemporary fiction and biblical commentary. Laced with humor and heartfelt self-disclosure, Liz's unique brand of "girlfriend theology" has helped women of all ages experience God's grace anew.